Practical Intelligence:
How to Think Critically, Deconstruct Situations, Analyze Deeply, and Never Be Fooled

By Patrick King
Social Interaction and Conversation Coach at
www.PatrickKingConsulting.com

Table of Contents

Practical Intelligence: *How to Think Critically, Deconstruct Situations, Analyze Deeply, and Never Be Fooled* 3

Table of Contents 5

Chapter 1. Look Beneath the Surface 7
- Curious as a Cat.. 15
- A Skeptic's View 24
- The Critical Thinker 32
- Paul-Elder Thinking 40

Chapter 2. Watch Yourself......................... 67
- Two Systems of Thought...................... 70
- Battling Biases... 80
- Logical Arguments 103

Chapter 3. Think in Models................... 117
- Models in Brief....................................... 127
- Process Versus Outcome 134
- Storytell in Reverse 142
- Separate Correlation from Causation 149

Chapter 4: Thought Divergence 161
- SCAMPER Method................................. 165
- Take, Borrow, Steal 178
- Thinking More "Plainly" 191

    Idea Box **196**

Chapter 5. The (Un)Limited Brain **203**
    Circadian Rhythms **207**
    Stress, Sleep, and Exercise **213**
    The Need for Less **225**
    Fuel Yourself **231**

Summary Guide **239**

Chapter 1. Look Beneath the Surface

Some of us are blessed with academic intelligence, otherwise known as pure book intelligence. This ability helps you in school, but it has limited applicability in the real world. It turns out there is just not that much use for memorizing equations and taking tests most of the time.

Others of us have kinesthetic intelligence, emotional intelligence, and even musical intelligence. You can guess what areas of life those help with.

But *practical intelligence* is sorely lacking these days. It's also known as common sense, seeing the world for what it is, and *how to think*. In reality, it turns out that *how* we navigate the world and approach it is far more important than what we actually know about it.

Practical intelligence is about taking in your surroundings, ascertaining what's happening, and then making the best decision for you with the information you've got. This might seem to be the most important of thinking skills, but it's also one that is never explicitly taught. We are mostly left to ourselves to figure it out, and this can easily explain a lot of the mental errors we observe people making on a daily basis.

Going out of business sale? Okay, I need to buy everything right now.

This news article makes an outrageous claim without a citation? Well, sounds about right, so I will now believe it with all my might.

If I feel something is true, then it must be true.

And so on. You may be able to spot these errors at the moment, but these thoughts occur automatically throughout our lives, and we certainly don't catch all of them. Let's take the first step into using our brains for good, instead of using them to fall into traps and follies. It's always about looking underneath the surface and stopping the assumption that you can trust what you see, hear, and feel.

We've all got that distant relative or long-lost friend who sends us occasional e-mails outlining the details of an off-the-rails conspiracy theory. This week, it's the outrageous, infuriating, and *"totally proven!"* theory that the government is using children's television shows to send secret messages to obey their orders. And unfortunately, you've opened this e-mail from your relative, even though you should know at this point that when something from this person is labeled "IMPORTANT!" it most certainly will not be.

"Look at this data from the National Alphabet Council!" they write. "It shows that Big Bird from *Sesame Street* triggers a part of your brain that responds positively to authority! It's all in his beak! Over 85 percent of all *Sesame Street* watchers report experiencing electrical seizures every time Big Bird appears onscreen! I learned all this from Jack Sprat's podcast *Under Attack!* Stop your kids from watching *Sesame Street* unless you want them to be lackeys to an authoritarian dictator!"

Something strikes you as . . . *fishy* about this particular story.

The National Alphabet Council? What is *that*? And all those kids reporting seizures? Geez, you know some people with kids. You'd think you would have heard about this by now. And isn't Jack Sprat that guy who claimed pasteurized milk makes schoolkids pledge allegiance to Satan?

All right, so you Google "National Alphabet Council." To your utter lack of surprise, there's no such organization with its own website. But you did find a link to a Snopes.com article that reveals the National Alphabet Council was used as a "source" to prove that *Green Eggs and Ham* was a Communist manifesto.

First off, this e-mail didn't pass the sniff test—something just seems *off* about it. Next, you don't find *any* data corroborating the reports on electrical seizures from kids watching *Sesame Street*. You find no evidence that Big Bird's beak is sending out coded messages to children. However, you do find something about Jack Sprat: an interview he gave with a major metropolitan newspaper in which he admits, "Look, I'm just an entertainer. I make people feel a certain way. If I believed half the stuff I talk about, I wouldn't be doing a show. I'd be curled up in the corner of my room, waiting for the world to end. Instead, I get a handsome paycheck!"

You send this information to your relative. They respond back, "Well, that's interesting. I haven't thought about that. But that Jack Sprat is so *passionate* about his beliefs, and he's a great communicator. I think I'll stick to what he says. Say, have you heard the Illuminati is monitoring your online dating profiles?"

Humans all want certainty. We want to be sure of our beliefs—uncertainty is an uncomfortable feeling that we try to eliminate every time we make a decision or plan an event. And we want it fast—now, if not sooner.

Many of us consider doubt and hesitation as roadblocks to getting things done or signs of insecurity in our thoughts. We've even been taught since we were young that *speed* of certainty is a sign of intelligence and solid thinking. As a result, we often race to get our beliefs affirmed by the first source we find and adopt them as proven truth.

This path presents a critical error in our natural thinking instincts, and it's a tendency we must veer away from for better, smarter thinking. *Certainty is more important than accuracy.* We tend to seek out confirmation that's more passionate than truthful. We're more impressed by someone on television mounting a fervent argument about an issue, instead of a calm, reasoning, boring person who simply lays out the facts as they are. If someone's acting intensely about their beliefs, we're inclined to think they must have the truth on their side, and we get swept up right along with them.

Practical intelligence is about seeking truth, not prioritizing removing *uncertainty* over establishing certainty. They aren't the same thing. Eliminating uncertainty means giving serious thought to what's causing doubt—in our opening short story, that would be looking up the National Alphabet Council to find out if they're on the up-and-up. Establishing certainty is simply glomming on to the first "fact" that soothes the uncomfortable feeling of uncertainty, insecurity, and simply *not being sure of something*.

This first chapter is about not accepting anything at face value, because face value tends to deceive in often intentional ways. It's about seeking the truth and nothing but the truth. You can imagine this might make you a pain in the butt to deal with, but it's really not about that. It's about the fact that every situation has at least some complexity and nuance underneath it. And if you keep digging, oftentimes, things are completely different from what they seemed at first glance.

Making this whole process harder is the fact that the brain loves certainty so much that it processes it as a *reward*. Uncertainty is perceived by the brain as a threat that needs to be extinguished. The sooner we can remove that threat with certainty, the better, no matter how shaky the certainty's foundation.

The most effective models of thinking help us quickly decipher and comprehend what's happening in our world. They make it easier to decode and interpret what we see and lead us to consider matters more thoroughly. Ultimately that course will be more rewarding than slap-dash validations of what we *prefer* to believe.

One helpful thought structure could be called "*strong opinions loosely held.*" This means being positive and assured about what you believe, but open-minded enough to hear out viewpoints that might challenge your own. It also means accepting that there's nothing weak or embarrassing about changing your mind. Doing so with a solid grip on the facts is actually a sign of your mental *strength*; merely agreeing with the crowd is the *real* weakness.

Of course this is easier said than done, what with our brains being hungry for assurance and anxious in the face of disbelief. But we can train our brains to go more deeply beyond appearances and uncover the hidden details we don't see at first glance.

Curious as a Cat

The most powerful tool we have in overcoming our desire for certainty and looking beneath the surface isn't pre-existing intelligence or judgment. It's simple curiosity.

All human knowledge—from discovering fire and the wheel to the theory of relativity—sprang from someone being curious. It came from a drive to know more about the nature of the world. Curiosity drives one to dive deeply into the nuts and bolts until they come to a solid comprehension about a subject or situation.

And when they get to that point, they're eager to learn *more*. It's a self-perpetuating trait; the more you have of it, the more you want it. And if you have enough of this one mindset, you will be well positioned for deeper thinking.

Curiosity is a direct path to practical intelligence. Pursuing your avenues of curiosity will help you learn and perceive things that other people won't. Developing your inquisitiveness is vital to building your knowledge and awareness. Every field of thought or knowledge, without a single exception, is easier to learn if you keep your curiosity front and forward. It's how you can naturally get to the heart of things and comprehend deeply.

But curiosity isn't automatic, and it's not something you can just will into existence. Furthermore, some of us are blocked from curiosity because of fear: we tend to have severe anxiety about the unknown, and that anxiety can be particularly high when we're about to *find out* about the unknown.

What we need to do is delve more deeply into the nature of curiosity to understand how it really works and how we can use it. It's a far more versatile tool than you might initially expect, and can help you think in smarter ways. Think of this as a preliminary mindset to digging beneath the surface effectively on any topic.

Most of us would think, understandably so, that being curious is just a simple matter of having a higher interest in learning things or having new experiences. When we say someone is "naturally curious," we usually mean they are motivated by this interest more so than other people. But in reality, there's a lot more to curiosity than simply having a strong desire to know more—people can become curious for quite a few distinctly different reasons.

Psychology professor Todd B. Kashdan from George Mason University spent a considerable amount of time researching the nature of human curiosity. Kashdan sought to nail down the diverse characteristics of curiosity into what he called "dimensions."

Kashdan conducted a study with over four hundred participants, each of whom answered three hundred personality questions. Analyzing the data he received, Kashdan developed a model of curiosity that identified *five* dimensions of curiosity. These aspects reveal how certain people are motivated to be curious in the first place. Knowing these dimensions and how they work might help you fire up your own curiosity engines. Kashdan's dimensions include:

1. Joyous exploration. When considering the nature of curiosity, this dimension is probably what we're picturing: the simple thrill of discovering and experiencing things we don't yet know about. The joyous explorer views new knowledge as a component of personal growth, which for them is its own reward. They're genuinely *excited* about reading all of Shakespeare's plays, trying sushi for the first time, or riding cross-country in a race car. Amassing a wealth of different experiences and knowledge simply makes them happy.

2. Deprivation sensitivity. This branch of curiosity, on the other hand, is more about anxiety. Someone working from this dimension feels apprehensive or nervous about their lack of information—being "deprived" of knowledge makes them uneasy. To reduce this pressure, they engage their curiosity. The deprivation sensitivity dimension comes into play when we're trying to solve a problem, getting up to speed with our comprehension, or considering complicated or difficult ideas.

For example, if you're balancing your bank accounts and find you've spent more than you have on record, you get a little nervous, which in turn makes you go through your receipts to see if you've missed anything. If you're taking a philosophy class and the material's going way over your head, you feel anxious about your abilities and study a little harder (if you haven't let fear stop you, that is). When you finally discover the information you're seeking, your discomfort will—theoretically—stop.

3. Stress tolerance. Whereas deprivation sensitivity relates to how uncomfortable one feels about *not* having certain knowledge, the stress tolerance dimension focuses on the uneasy feelings that can come from *getting* that knowledge or taking on a new experience. A person with high stress tolerance in their pursuits is more likely to follow their curiosity. On the other hand, someone who can't deal with the uncertainty, disorder, or doubt that arises when exploring new ideas or having new experiences is less likely to let curiosity lead them.

Take two people who have never been on a roller coaster before and are in line to do so at an amusement park. Both of them are at least a little nervous about it because it's a new thing for them. One of them is more willing to confront their fears—they've done so before with other things and have always survived—so they're able to fight through their anxieties and get onboard. The other one, though, lets their fear reduce them into a quivering mass of exposed nerves. They have to take the chicken exit and miss out on the roller coaster.

The first person clearly has a higher ability to tolerate stress, can go past their fears, and will follow their curiosity for a new experience. As for the second person, well, let's hope they *really* like the merry-go-round, because that's pretty much all they can handle.

4. Social curiosity. This dimension of curiosity is simply the desire to know what's going on with other people: what they're thinking, doing, and saying. We indulge this curiosity by interacting with or watching others. We'll have a conversation with a friend because we're interested in a movie they just saw, or we want to hear their opinions on current events, or we just have to share in the latest gossip they've heard.

Social curiosity can also come from a more detached point of observation. A great example of this is people-watching in a crowded place, like a bus stop or Central Park. We might see a couple having a spat, or a couple kids playing a game they just made up, or a man walking his pet duck. (It happens.) Based on what they're doing or saying, we might form certain judgments or opinions about how they really are or how they behave in a more private situation. Curiosity drives us to study them.

5. Thrill-seeking. This aspect is similar to the stress tolerance dimension, except a thrill-seeker doesn't just tolerate risk — they actually *like* it. A thrill-seeker is more than happy to place themselves in harm's way just so they can gain more experience. For them, it's worth the gamble of physical jeopardy, social disavowal, or financial ruin just to have an adventure or encounter something new.

For a thrill-seeking example, look no further than Richard Branson, the hugely successful entrepreneur. He's tried to balloon around the world. He's tried to race a boat across the Atlantic. He's stood valiantly in the path of oncoming storms that destroyed everything else in the immediate vicinity. Branson, in fact, claims to have had *seventy-six* "near-death experiences," including one where he went over the handlebars of the bicycle he was riding. Branson escaped with only minor injuries as he watched his bike go off the edge of a cliff. Clearly, Branson feels extremely comfortable in situations where there's an element of danger. That's your thrill-seeker.

For the joyous explorer and thrill-seeker, curiosity is pretty easy and automatically generated. It's the same for the socially curious, depending on the situation and who surrounds them. For these three dimensions, curiosity is a welcome and comfortable condition. If you're aware of the positive benefits you are getting from something, it's easier to indulge in them. But we may not always feel that way, so we can't really depend on it.

If you're resistant to curiosity, you might serve yourself by considering the origins of your anxiety. If you're feeling awkward about not being "in the know" or left out of the loop, you could use that motivation to drive you to amend that situation (deprivation sensitivity). If you're unable to fight through your fears, you might consider ways to rationalize them and get stronger (stress tolerance). Overall, we just want to understand what drives us toward and, conversely, what prevents us from embodying a curious mindset. Knowing the driving motivation helps.

For the remainder of this chapter, we'll look at techniques and approaches that can at least *simulate* a sense of curiosity to help bring you to new knowledge and experience—therefore helping you go beyond the surface level and get to the bottom of things.

We can't all naturally think, "Hey, what does that *really* mean?" so these mental models will help you reach that point methodically.

A Skeptic's View

Skepticism is a model to truly understand what you're looking at and gain the truthful view of it. The word "skepticism" is frequently misunderstood, sometimes being labeled an undesirable trait. When someone says they're skeptical about a certain thing, they might ruffle the feathers of somebody else who thinks they're just letting their negativity get in the way. Why'd they have to ruin all the fun with their skepticism?

Some people use the word "skeptical" interchangeably with the word "cynical"—but there's a world of difference between the two. Except for both trains of thought involving a measure of disbelief, they couldn't be more different.

A skeptic approaches everything from a standpoint of reason and learning; they're open-minded but picky about requiring evidence. The cynic, however, distrusts any viewpoints they don't already agree with. They're firm and fixed in their beliefs. They believe everything in life will progress in a certain way and there's no point in questioning it. Even hard, verifiable evidence may not sway their beliefs.

Cynicism is dangerous because it implies there are no answers to anything in life. A cynic believes that matters have already been determined and there's no point in challenging them. Cynicism shuts down investigation and discourages interest. That's dangerous because it leads to hopelessness. Skepticism, on the other hand, has a positive goal of discovering real truth.

A skeptic seeks to find irrefutable truth, or as close as they can get to it. This by definition involves going beneath the surface and determining what's really in front of you. The word itself derives from the Greek *skeptikos*, which translates to "inquiring" or "looking around." The mission of a skeptic is to question. The skeptic's mind is trained to look for the basic facts, impartial to any bias or agenda. This is probably an unnatural way for most of us to be thinking, but it can shed light on how much you leave uncovered.

Skeptics don't settle for having blind faith or wishing truth into existence. They don't *want* to burst anyone's bubble, but neither do they want to fill someone up with false confidence. They just want to understand, and they do not discriminate between the conclusions that might surface. They are the impartial judge of a criminal court, with similar standards and adherence to intellectual honesty. They see things in only black and white, as you also must. There can be no wiggle room.

Skeptics operate only on *evidence*. They must have proof that the assertions of other people actually work or are completely true. They can't accept facts simply at face value. Before a skeptic can decide something's real, they need to see confirmation in the form of data or consistently repeated results. The mere fact that someone just "heard somebody say something" is nowhere close to being evidence. That's merely an anecdote, and the plural of anecdotes is *also* not evidence.

A healthy skeptic always considers and questions the source of certain information—and no matter how high up or acclaimed that source may be, they're still subject to being confirmed by evidence. A source may have impeccable credentials, a gleaming reputation, and considerable fame or authority. All of that's great. *They still need to have evidence.*

Skepticism will feel more satisfying the more you use it, and you'll be less prone to flawed thinking, counterfeit facts, and weak arguments. Just make sure you don't become an annoying pedant with this newfound power of scrutiny you've found. Skepticism is more of a mindset of withholding judgment until you are sure the truth is plain to see.

This pursuit of truth and reality might echo something you're already familiar with, the *scientific method*. Indeed, skeptics resemble scientists more than anything else for their strict standards of proof. The scientific method is a time-proven process for gathering information that scientists have used for centuries to test their theories. It works by putting observations and assumptions to scrutiny to ensure that the truth is discovered. For instance, if someone makes an observation that it grows colder at night, there would be no way of proving this to be truth unless data was collected during daytime and nighttime and compared.

The scientific method is generally considered to consist of five stages: asking a question, constructing a hypothesis, testing by experimentation, analysis of results, and forming a conclusion. In fact, this process exactly mirrors skepticism. An assertion without evidence or fact is as good as an opinion, and certainly nothing close to truth.

Thus, in order to put everyday statements to the test, you're going to have to conduct an experiment, collect data, and analyze results empirically. Skepticism leads you down a line of inquiry and discovery that cuts out the assumptions and opens doors of truth.

Now that we've established that "skepticism" isn't a dirty word and is a hallmark of thinking smarter, how does one actually use it to evaluate the relative truthfulness of a claim? Here's a skeletal guideline for how to approach a topic with appropriate skepticism.

1. Intake the statement. Fully absorb the meaning and implications of the claim after it's been made. Even if it sounds ridiculous to you at first hearing, at least pretend that it's a serious and meaningful belief. Give your source the benefit of the doubt for this one brief step. This will allow you to give it the attention it deserves, if even just to poke holes in it. When we dismiss, we don't pay attention.

2. Question the source. Consider the viability of the source of the information. Then, consider the possible intentions of such a source. If it's a publication, media outlet, or website, gauge its reputation and agenda—there are plenty of legitimate-looking sources that aren't above distorting or stretching the truth to serve an agenda. If it's a friend, relative, or acquaintance, ask them to tell you where *they* got the information (without devolving into a heated argument, if possible).

3. Search for supporting arguments or information. If a certain claim has "gone public," there's probably ample information supporting it that you can easily find on the web. Find the arguments in favor of the statement you're researching—and again, question the sources as you go.

4. Search for opposing arguments or information. Repeat Step 3, but this time, look for statements or sources that either deny or criticize the information you're looking up. Be aware of the possibility of confirmation bias on your part while doing this step—don't discount opposing views or gravitate toward unreliable sources just because they'll back up your own beliefs. Give yourself a higher standard of truth.

5. Question your findings logically. Here's where you put together what you've learned and weigh the likelihood of the statement being true or false. I like to write things down as a way of thinking through them, and you can do that by listing pros and cons, making a mind map, or writing a persuasive essay to yourself. Or you can simply do some heavy contemplation in your head without writing anything down. Remember, you are seeking evidence, not certainty, and you don't need an explicit answer. You just want to look beneath the surface. Wherever the evidence points is where you look.

If you find the original claim viable, then you agree. If you've found too much doubt or contradictory evidence, you disagree. If you've seen compelling evidence for *both* sides and can't reconcile it right now, you can decide to leave it for the time being. Again, what's important is truth, not certainty.

The Critical Thinker

Critical thinking is the act of delaying gratification in lieu of accuracy and a three-dimensional understanding of the nuances presented to you. It's not terribly popular as a way of navigating life, but it's how you are going to learn to look beneath the surface of any statement.

The goal of critical thinking isn't to produce a quick, easily digestible answer. In fact, it's not even to provide any certifiable conclusion whatsoever. Instead, the point of critical thinking is to make a topic more transparent. The essence of critical thinking centers not on answering questions but on questioning answers. The approach is different, but the end goal is the same as skepticism's—to find the truth of the matter.

Rather than provide a rock-solid, inarguable conviction, critical thinking expands your viewpoint and gives you several ways to look at a situation or problem. It gets you past the external noise and easy answers to show you the whole scope of a circumstance or issue. It allows you to have a discussion about information or a topic, even if only with yourself. That's where you'll learn more than what meets the eye.

The questions you use in critical thinking go beyond standard "just the facts, ma'am" inquiries. Instead, they challenge the answerer to probe the reasons for a subject's importance, its origins, relevance, and countering or alternative beliefs. They can be applied to any subject—even, with some adaptation, scientific or mathematical principles. The goal isn't to get you to agree or disagree with a given doctrine, but just to understand the totality of its meaning.

Let's try an example: *the theory of gravity*. All you need to know is that it is generally one of the laws of physics that govern our planet and the universe as we know it. We might think we know what it is, but subjecting it to a line of critical thinking questions would probably uncover the fact that it's not what you first thought.

Here are some questions you could use to critically evaluate the topic. I'm not going to attempt to answer them, because last time I checked, I wasn't a physicist. But I did look up enough to form some decent questions, and the main point of this exercise is to show how they can be phrased:

What makes the theory of gravity important? This question, obviously, seeks out why the theory of gravity deserves to be talked about.

Which details of the theory of gravity are important and why? This question gets down into the specific elements of the theory of gravity and how they affect certain factors of a body's motion.

What differentiates the theory of gravity from other theories? Why? This question seeks to discover why the idea does or does not have special significance.

What is an example of the theory of gravity? This question seeks to gain understanding through a concrete example.

What are the differences between the theory of gravity and other physics laws? This query compares two different models and allows you to understand what sets one model apart from the other.

How is the theory of gravity related to quantum physics? This question sets up a description of how the subject relates to other existing knowledge.

What evidence can you provide for or against the theory of gravity? This question forces acknowledgment of both positive and negative aspects of the subject. Each subject or topic has weaknesses and strengths regarding its applicability and universality.

What patterns do you notice in the theory of gravity? This helps you search out repetitive elements and cause-and-effect relationships, which almost always indicate importance.

What are the advantages and disadvantages of the theory of gravity? This question sets up another comparison between the possible effects of the theory of gravity.

When might the theory of gravity be most useful and why? This question looks for an example of how the concept is used in the real world and can affect your life.

What criteria would you use to assess whether the theory of gravity is accurate? This question seeks how to establish hard proof that a concept is working or not and introduces the concept of specific metrics.

What information would you need to make a decision about the theory of gravity? This question addresses the conditions in which Keynesian models can thrive and what contextual information is important.

Do you agree that the theory of gravity works? Why or why not? This question encourages you to use your own reasoning to judge the merit of a certain concept.

How could you create or design a new model of the theory of gravity? Explain your thinking. This question urges you to reimagine the concept in accordance with your own ideas and project how they could work in the future.

Whew. That's a lot of questions. It's only a fraction of the many sides and angles from which you can examine any given issue. None of them are answered in definitive terms, nor can they be. But their open-ended nature encourages you to pursue the facts from an objective standpoint. Is this beginning to sound circular and repetitive? It can indeed be a never-ending and tedious exercise, but if you keep the purpose of discovery and perspective at the forefront, it becomes more meaningful.

At this point, you may have used all your answers to formulate a theory or conclusion—or you've come across conclusions from others that address *their* interpretation of what the facts mean. But as with the questions you've just asked, the ideas you come across (even your own) should *also* be subjected to the same kind of inquisition as to whether the conclusions are sound and hold up.

The first few questions should address the structure of the conclusion, whether it comes from a sound basis in reasoning. A second set of questions focuses instead on the quality of the conclusions and supporting arguments. We can see this through the same example of our theory of gravity model:

What are the issues and conclusions of the theory of gravity? This question addresses the foundation of the theory—the problem it was trying to solve—and what the answers are.

What are the reasons for your conclusions? A well-worded conclusion will list out the facts being used to support it. This question identifies what those facts are. And it's crucial to separate facts from anecdotes or *feelings*.

What assumptions are you using in your theory? If there are any variable factors being used when the conclusion is formed, it's important to ferret them out. For instance, generally, the theory of gravity assumes that the laws of relativity apply and a quantum singularity is nowhere nearby.

The next two questions seek to expose the shortcomings of thought that may have compromised the finding of the conclusions:

Are there fallacies in the reasoning? This question seeks out any inaccuracies, mistakes, or outright falsehoods in any of the reasons given.

How good is the evidence? This is how you check that the supporting facts behind the conclusion are airtight, from legitimate sources, and not discolored by bias or misinformation.

There's a chance that these questions might raise even *more* questions instead of answering all your inquiries. But again, that's the main point of this line of interrogation: to create a three-dimensional view of the topic you're investigating and not just stop at the first answer that looks "certain." Just because something is certain does not mean it is truthful.

But wait—critical thinking can go even more deeply, and we look to the Paul-Elder model for that. This approach is really going deeper into the rabbit hole, so to speak.

Paul-Elder Thinking

As might be apparent by now, improving the quality of your thinking, your mental agility and your intelligence is never something that happens by accident, but rather something that you develop consciously and deliberately. Paul-Elder's framework for critical thinking is an extremely useful tool for training yourself intellectually and improving the *quality* of your thinking. This goes far beyond the set of questions we examined previously, and sheds a light into an entirely different mode of thought.

Thinking, as a function, can take on many characteristics. Just as physical movement can be graceful and in good form, thinking can be ordered and "correct" in a similar way—or else clumsy and inelegant! By having intellectual standards, we establish a goal for the quality of thought we strive to achieve, and a big part of this is developing the skill and habit of critical thinking.

There are three main components to this framework:

1. The elements of thought or reasoning
2. The intellectual standards that should be applied to the elements of reasoning and
3. The intellectual traits of a critical thinker.

Let's begin with the first component. What are the elements of reasoning? Paul-Elder invites us to consider the units of the thought process itself, and assess them and their function. The authors proposed eight structural elements of reasoning:

1. Purpose
2. Questions
3. Point of view
4. Information
5. Inferences
6. Concepts
7. Implications
8. Assumptions

The first, *purpose*, is otherwise called your goal, objective or intention. A good critical thinker will be crystal clear on their purpose. In other words, what are you really trying to do here, and why? Does your goal need refinement, or expansion?

Another element is *the question itself*, the problem at hand or the issue being explored. Heisenberg famously claimed, "What we observe is not nature itself, but nature exposed to our method of questioning." Essentially, the quality of your inquiry matters, and will shape the rest of your critical thinking. To assess this element, ask yourself exactly what question you're trying to answer—and how you're stating that question. Could you frame it differently? What kind of question is it, and could it be simplified? What form will the answer take? Is it really a collection of several smaller questions?

Critical thinking also entails *gathering information*. If you've refined your question properly, you are able to gather data that is relevant to it, and ignore data that isn't. Ask yourself whether the data you're gathering is not just relevant, but also sufficient—i.e., is there enough of it? Is it accurate, and where did it come from? Is there some information you're missing? When you judge a piece of data as relevant, how exactly are you making that appraisal?

This will seamlessly lead you to another component, *inference*. You take in the data in front of you and draw conclusions from it. You interpret a set of facts to come to some conclusive statement about it. However, to check that you're doing this correctly, you need to make sure your inferences actually flow logically from the evidence at hand. Does your interpretation make sense, or have you overlooked another possible angle? How did you reach your conclusion, and is it sound—i.e., did you make any unfounded assumptions? Inferences should be no more and no less than the data suggests. Here's the moment when you weigh up alternatives and question your assumptions.

From this flows another component, *concepts*. These are the theories, ideas, models, principles and laws we construct for ourselves to better help us understand the data we see. Again, concepts should be "justifiable," which means they should be appropriate to the data, not go above or beyond it. Think carefully about your hypothesis, your claims and your assumptions. Try to find the core thread or principle and ask whether it's sufficiently clear, simple and relevant. Models are only good so long as they accurately reflect reality and allow us to make predictions. Does your model/theory do this? Why or why not?

Assumptions are another component we've already mentioned. These are ideas we take for granted—consciously or unconsciously—even though there may not strictly be evidence for them. Ask what "obvious" pieces of information you're relying on or haven't properly looked at. What is being taken as a given, and what have you glanced over as unimportant? Is it? Look closely at all the steps you took to reach your conclusions or theories and ask if they're strictly supported by fact.

Implications and consequences are another component. If you settle on an idea or "truth," then some other ideas or truths will naturally and logically follow from the first. Actions have consequences, and thoughts have implications. Have you considered all of yours? What naturally follows if you do/claim something? What are the likely implications of taking your position or making your particular claim?

Finally, the eighth component is *point of view*, which is essentially your own unique perspective or orientation. Nobody has the privilege of a completely neutral frame of reference, so it's worth considering what your position is, and how it affects your reasoning. What are you focusing on and why? Is there another alternative perspective worth considering? Is your view reasonable—or does it ignore or amplify certain things? Consider how your point of view interacts with your assumptions and your conclusions about what's in front of you. Does it contrast with others'? Are you giving yourself sufficient opportunity to challenge your orientation, or reconsider points of view that may be limiting you or causing you confusion or distress?

As you can see, each of these components makes up the complex and ever-changing process of our thinking. But without conscious awareness of *how* these components are working and interacting, the quality of our thought is unlikely to be high. You may run wild with unfounded assumptions, draw faulty conclusions or start extrapolating from incomplete data to prove a poorly conceived theory that is only backed up by partial, low-quality data. And you might not be aware that you are doing it!

Now, the whole reason for understanding these elements (the first part of the framework) is so that you can appraise and improve upon them using your intellectual standards (the second part). In asking some of the questions we have above, we've seen how it's possible to challenge and explore each of these components. Paul-Elder had a more formalized way of doing this, which they called their "universal intellectual standards." These determine the *quality* of the reasoning, acting as a guide for thinking. You may perform some of these questions or appraisals deliberately at first, but the goal is to make them more habitual and automatic with time.

There are nine standards in total, and they can each in turn be applied to the elements listed above:

1. Clarity
2. Accuracy
3. Precision
4. Relevance
5. Depth
6. Breadth
7. Logic
8. Significance
9. Fairness

The first standard is *clarity*. To clarify is to cut down on confusion or vagueness, for instance if you can elaborate on a claim, provide an example, or if you can paraphrase or simplify what you're saying. Often, what seems like a great idea is really just a noisy, busy one that falls apart once you try to streamline it.

Accuracy is the standard of veracity. In other words, is it true? How could you tell? When checking a claim or a piece of information's truth, we also have to consider the source and motivation of the evidence itself. Really ask why you have reason to believe this idea is true—or not. Is it better understood as a theory or opinion?

The standard of *precision* is also important. It's about specificity. Good thinking is about exact statements that are clear and focused. Are you being too general? Sometimes, good critical thinking means getting into the details of things to find *exactly* what you're saying.

Relevance is a standard already mentioned. This is not a value judgment, or a personal opinion, but rather an assessment of whether your thought actually has anything to do with your stated aim. It's necessary to bear the original question in mind, and keep comparing your questions, data and interpretations against it. Is what you're thinking about actually helping the issue at hand?

Depth is the standard that concerns levels of complexity. Are you thinking in too shallow a fashion? Have you properly considered the difficulties and complexities of the issue at hand? This standard allows you to fully comprehend the real scope of the question, and the extent to which you're trying to solve it.

Similarly, *breadth* is a question not of the complexities and difficulties of an issue, but rather its natural boundaries. Have you considered enough other perspectives? Could the way you're thinking be expanded to include more? Here's where you weigh alternative points of view and expand the edges of your own.

Logic is an obvious standard that is harder to apply than it seems. It can be difficult to pick apart, but ask yourself whether what you're thinking strictly *makes sense*. If your thinking was an argument, would each premise flow naturally from the previous one? Does your claim actually follow from the evidence at hand? Are you solving the problem in the right terms? This standard is about making sure that the elements of your thinking are actually cohering soundly.

The standard of *significance* is, in a way, about focus. Look carefully at the information you are choosing to focus on, and ask whether it really is the most significant aspect of the issue at hand. Try to find the central issue of the matter and pay it proportional attention. Are you getting sidetracked by relatively insignificant details? Look closely to sift through and filter out only what is most important.

Finally, the standard of *fairness* is significant, although a little tricky to get a handle on. Here, you ask yourself whether your thinking is "justifiable." A good critical thinker considers the thinking of others, and the purpose they're working toward. This standard is the closest to a moral aspect—are you actually using your intellect clearly and honorably, or are you merely attempting to win an argument or manipulate data in order to get what you want from the situation? This standard asks that we are being reasonable and mature in the way we think, and to carefully consider the consequences.

Sadly, many people mistake intellectual rigor for a blood sport, or think that developing critical thinking is merely a fancy way to assert intellectual dominance over others and win arguments. This is why it's crucial to consistently question your own position, your own intentions and your own limitations. A critical thinker is not someone who is really good at being right, or showing their intellectual prowess. Rather, a critical thinker is someone who has trained themselves to be comfortable with being wrong, and who can use their cognitive processes not just to confirm what they already know or wish was the case, but rather to enlighten themselves and reveal new avenues of thinking that might otherwise be hidden by sloppy or unexamined thought.

This leads us to the third and final part of the framework, which is the intellectual traits that Elder saw as belonging to those who have mastered critical thinking. In successfully applying our intellectual standards to the elements of reasoning, we fine-tune our mental apparatus and become better thinkers, period. Those who have developed the habit (and it's a *habit*, not a static personality trait) of critical thinking display certain characteristics, and in turn can do well to cultivate the characteristics themselves.

These traits include:

1. Intellectual humility
2. Intellectual courage
3. Fair-mindedness.
4. Intellectual empathy (i.e. the ability to not just pay lip service to other

points of view, but to actually deeply consider them as alternatives to their own view)
5. Confidence in one's own reasoning
6. Intellectual autonomy, i.e. the ability to "think for oneself"
7. Intellectual perseverance, i.e. the ability to push on with a confusing, unpopular or difficult concept.
8. Integrity

Though it's helpful to bear these qualities in mind when developing your own mental capacity, they are better understood as emergent qualities that come from the consistent application of intellectual standards to the elements of your own reasoning. In other words, we can idealize the strong, toned physiques of professional athletes, but we can only achieve that for ourselves with diligent, consistent training.

People who make critical thinking a part of their daily lives will learn to formulate their problems clearly and concisely, and will *watch themselves* think about solutions, asking whether the data they're using is relevant, sufficient, and logical. They'll keep asking questions (primarily of themselves!) and test any conclusions they come to against both intellectual standards and their own objectives. They will take great pains to make sure they don't accept faulty interpretations, or fail to consider alternatives. They are simultaneously open-minded and geared toward refining and concluding. They are above all curious, and want to find the best way to satisfy this curiosity—not to be "right," but for the satisfaction of cultivating knowledge about themselves and the world. In all this, they don't lose sight of the context in which they operate, and they know how to communicate with others, even in complex situations or where viewpoints differ.

Let's consider a few examples of how this entire process works together. Imagine you're at a get-together of friends and are introduced to someone new, and you strike up a conversation with them. You compliment them on their cool shirt, and they tell you how surprisingly cheap it was and what a good deal they got on it. You make a lighthearted comment about how it was probably made in a sweatshop somewhere, like so much of our clothing today. The other person laughs but says, "Well, let's hope not. But, not all sweatshops are bad."

You gear up to disagree, and share what you know about the issue: that sweatshops for major clothing labels are responsible for some of the worst human rights violations in the world, and exploit third-world countries only to make massive profits for already wealthy corporations. In fact, you're surprised that this person doesn't know this, and soon you're embroiled in a heated discussion.

If you were a practiced critical thinker, however, you would pause here and practice some humility, becoming genuinely curious about your new friend's position and claims, and what information they have to back them up. You would be aware of your own emotional investment in the issue, and would start to question your own perspective rather than jump in with an argument based on assumptions.

Throughout your conversation, you ask thoughtful but focused questions to try to understand their point of view—and your own. Why do they think that some sweatshops are not bad? Where did they get their information? You practice fairness in your thinking. You hold off on making a conclusion until you've gathered the facts.

After a long conversation, you discover that this person comes from a country where "sweatshops" pay workers in one week what they'd receive doing a month's worth of any other work. You learn that many previously destitute people are able to work and support their families because of these clothing manufacturers—and your friend comes from one of these families. You learn that although sweatshops do indeed subject workers to horrific conditions, they also happen to be the best option for many in some countries—a complicated piece of information you didn't possess before.

You quickly realize that, sweatshops being an issue you've never really taken the time to consider, there's more to it than you thought. You also realize that, compared to your friend, you actually possess less information about this topic, and are not even sure where your impressions about it come from. You leave the conversation with a renewed interest in better understanding the politics of your friend's home country, and are grateful for the opportunity to have questioned your knee-jerk, unexamined opinions about a very complex topic.

In this example, the elements under question include:

- Point of view (how your unique perspective affected your conclusions)
- Information (whether you have sufficient knowledge to draw conclusions, or are missing key pieces of information)

- Concepts (the popular "zero sum" model of cheap labor in developing countries)
- Assumptions (An obvious one: that nobody really *wants* to work in a sweatshop, right?)

Intellectual standards can then be applied to these in turn:

- Depth and breadth could be applied to your point of view (i.e. is yours really the only viable one?)
- You can use some standards for good information (Is it sufficient and high quality? Where did you get your opinion from?)
- You can apply the same standards you have for information to your concepts (Is your model of sweatshops accurate? Does it really reflect the reality this other person is sharing with you?)
- The standard of accuracy and significance can be applied to the assumptions you've made (Simply,

are they true? Have you been focusing on the wrong thing?)

All the above can be considered together with the critical thinking traits of intellectual humility and fair-mindedness (i.e. considering the fact that winning the argument is not worth offending and alienating your conversation partner.)

Failing to understand the elements of your own thinking (your point of view, the data you have, the assumptions) or work hard to improve their quality by applying intellectual standards (asking about the logic, veracity, relevance and depth of your thought processes) may have taken this conversation in a completely different direction. It could have well turned into an argument, especially if instead of challenging your assumptions and realizing you were coming to conclusions off of incomplete data, you assumed the other person was ignorant and it was your job to educate them.

Though you still think it's not a good idea to buy "fast fashion," you have a more nuanced understanding of the issue than you did before. Because of your critical thinking, you *learned* something and improved your own intellectual abilities in the process. I'm sure you can agree that is more satisfying in the long run than the mere feeling of having "won" the argument!

Let's take a look at a more concrete example. As a clothing manufacturer, you're interested in using a newly developed cotton polyester blend that will be cheaper than your current fabric. But you have concerns about its quality and how well it will work with your machines, so you do some trial runs with sample fabric to test its performance in the factory.

Already, you have worked to form a *concept* (an experiment to test the new fabric) from which you intend to draw *inferences* (if it works in the experiment, it will work on a larger scale) for a stated *purpose* (to save money on fabric). To all of these elements of reasoning you can then apply a few intellectual standards. You ask whether you're being *accurate* in your measurement of the fabric performance. You ask whether the cost of the fabric is truly the only parameter to consider, or whether other things you're not thinking of could jeopardize your stated aim (i.e., you apply questions of *depth* and *breadth*).

You notice that you *want* a particular outcome (you are aware of your own point of view and see how this affects the questions you ask) but try hard to conduct the experiment neutrally. When the experiment shows that the new fabric gets jammed in one kind of sewing machine, you use logic to extrapolate to an appropriate conclusion: the fabric is incompatible with one type of machine, but that doesn't logically follow that *every* type of machine will have the same problem. And so it goes.

Perhaps you notice, however, that not all of the standards have been applied here—for example, the question of *fairness* is not considered, and there is only a very narrow view of the question (lack of *depth* and *breadth*), with a very limited understanding of *consequences*. The company may switch to the new fabric, only to discover that it washes poorly and that customers are so unsatisfied with it after purchase that within a few months, repeat custom drops significantly, completely cancelling out any small gains made in using the cheaper fabric.

Here, a critical thinker would notice the problem, update their mental model and make a point to remember this the next time they face a decision similar to this one. They would recognize that a few of their underlying premises were not sound—i.e., the idea that the clothing cost and whether it worked with the machines were the *only* parameters to consider.

Critical thinking can be applied on grand scales to big decisions like these, or in smaller situations like the conversation we saw at the get-together. You could apply critical thinking every time you use your brain—which, luckily, is pretty much continuously. The first step is to become aware of the various elements of your thinking. Your goals, your limitations, the "map" of reality you are using. But the next step is to take responsibility for these elements, and apply intellectual standards to improve them.

Is the way you're thinking clear? Logical? Fair? Are you focusing on the right things, and have you properly understood your goal? Eventually, critical thinking becomes more automatic. This doesn't mean that you are never wrong, or that you suddenly become a super-intelligent mega-mind. Rather, you are taking conscious control of your own mental and intellectual machinery, and using it to its highest potential.

You may still be wrong, you may still feel confused and you may still miss or misunderstand huge amounts of information out there, even though you explicitly try not to. However, making mistakes for a critical thinker is not a problem—it's merely more "grist for the mill," and can be fed back in and processed again, this time with the privilege of having updated your concepts, sharpened your goals and verified your claims. In essence, critical thinking is not really about *what* you think, but rather *how* you're thinking about it. Focus on improving the quality of the process, and the content of your thoughts will naturally improve as well.

Takeaways:

- Practical intelligence is another way of saying common sense, but we all know that common sense truly is not so common. One of the key lessons to learn with practical intelligence is that nothing is what it seems at first glance. The world doesn't readily reveal itself nakedly to you, so it's up to you to look beneath the surface to understand what you see. We want to do this, but we are too often driven by certainty and speed instead of actual truth.

- The first and most natural way to probe below the surface is through cultivating curiosity. There are five types of curiosity, each of which can be said to be a motivation for asking questions: joyous exploration, deprivation sensitivity, stress tolerance, social curiosity, and thrill-seeking. However, curiosity will rarely come easily or naturally, especially about things that we don't have an innate interest in. So we need to generate that same approach through other methods.

- One methodical way to seek truth and simulate curiosity is by embracing skepticism. No, it's not about being *cynical* or simply refusing to believe what people tell you. Rather, it's refusing to blindly believe what people tell you, and requiring evidence and facts. In this way, a skeptic is quite similar to a scientist utilizing the scientific method. No answer is required here, and only understanding is sought. Skepticism requires slowing down your thoughts and thinking like a scientist.

- Finally, we come to critical thinking. Critical thinking is concerned with questioning answers rather than asking questions. It seeks to take nothing at face value and provide a three-dimensional and nuanced view of a topic or stance. Without that, you are by definition jumping to conclusions or relying on someone else's word—an opinion without inquiry is a weak one. We can practice critical thinking through a series of questions, but we can also go a level deeper by running inquiries and thoughts through the Paul-Elder framework of critical thinking. This involves three components that ultimately work together to build a bulletproof thinking process: (1) elements of thought and reasoning, (2) intellectual standards to be applied to these elements, and (3) the cultivation and eventual development of intellectual traits.

Chapter 2. Watch Yourself

In the first chapter of this book, we discussed how our psyches are pre-programmed to make the wrong judgments about what we see in a world that often isn't what it seems to be. We also talked about how skepticism and critical thinking can help us vanquish those errors in discernment.

In this chapter, we'll face many of the same issues, but this time, we'll start by talking about how *biological* factors can lead us to the same errors in judgment. We are biologically programmed to lack self-awareness in many ways, and when we don't know what is driving us, we will often be driven right off the cliff. A doctor probably shouldn't operate unless they know the true causes of an illness; we should understand the baseline that our brains operate from in order to properly move forward.

The brain seems like a complex machine, and in many ways, it is. But you *could* view it as nothing more than an electrical network housed inside your skull. Information goes from neuron to neuron via electrical impulses that flicker across the synapses. Nothing more than trains and relay stations.

Just like the electric currents flowing from power outlets, the brain impulses that control our thoughts prefer to follow the path of least resistance. The brain maintains these easy passageways of thought for maximum effectiveness and speed. This means that the more you think about a certain thing, the more the brain isolates and reinforces the path that thought travels along—therefore making it easier to think about that thing again in the future.

That's both good and bad news. It's good in that refining those thought pathways makes certain mental tasks easier to accomplish. It's helpful for creating good habits and reinforcing positivity. But it's bad because if we latch on to negative or errant thoughts, they can become our default thought patterns, and this can be difficult to avoid. This is exactly where *bad* habits come from, and it's why even though we logically know the spider won't eat us, we can't bear to face it. Our biological makeup overrules smart and clear thinking, and in effect robs us of our common sense and practical intelligence. Our brains become wired for flawed thinking, and this chapter uncovers how that happens and how to reverse it.

You *can* take measures to counteract the faulty thoughts that take hold in the brain, and gain clarity of thought. It takes some dedicated and deliberate monitoring of our mental processes and understanding how they work. We call this practice *metacognition*—very simply, thinking about our thinking and *watching yourself* dispassionately and objectively.

Two Systems of Thought

The brain is a wonder of biology. However, just like all our body parts, it gets exhausted when it's overused. To prevent exhaustion, the brain regulates some of its processes so it can conserve the energy needed to power all its functions. This means it's always seeking shortcuts, so we don't have to think every last thing through, thereby conserving energy. In reality, the brain ends up cutting corners and ignoring important information in the interest of saving precious energy. In past eras, this was helpful because it allowed us to prioritize survival instincts above all else. But it's much less useful to us now.

The brain's search for shortcuts has led to two systems of thought—one focused on speed and conservation of energy, and the other on accuracy and analysis. This is something we must be vigilant about, especially when we are introduced to new information or concepts. The brain would rather save energy for survival situations, but little does it realize that it can actually cause them through flawed thinking.

This concept was popularized by professor Daniel Kahneman in his seminal book *Thinking, Fast and Slow*. Through a series of experiments, Kahneman developed a model that explains the separate processes the brain uses to absorb and react to various bits of information, imaginatively titled *System 1 thinking* and *System 2 thinking*.

System 1 is "fast" thinking. This mode is automatic and instinctive. It's what we use when we happen upon a situation that we're familiar with and don't need to process that much, like recognizing a friend, riding a bicycle, or doing single-digit math calculations. Since it's intuitive, System 1 thinking is also associated with emotional reactions, like crying or laughing when seeing an old photograph.

The main facet of System 1 thinking is effortlessness. It doesn't require anything in the way of analysis or consideration, instead using a framework of associations that we've already experienced time and time again. System 1 is a series of mental shortcuts—called *heuristics*—that help us decode situations very quickly (more on those soon). And because there's little time or effort used in System 1 thinking, it expends less energy and isn't terribly exhausting. You're not going to need a list of pros and cons to make decisions with System 1. Although System 1 is quicker, it's aimed at doing the *fast* thing versus the *right* thing.

System 2, on the other hand, is "slow" thinking. This style is much more contemplative and analytical, and it's generally used when we're absorbing a new experience or learning. It's employed for any situation that requires more mental labor and effort. System 2 controls decision-making in events that could result in high consequences, like choosing a college, buying a new car, or quitting your job.

You also use System 2 when you're doing something that needs more focus or effort, like driving through a foggy night, striving to hear someone speak in a noisy room, trying to recall a conversation you had a few weeks ago, or learning a complex school subject that's new to you. Skepticism and critical thinking, like the kind we discussed earlier in this book, fall under System 2.

Whereas System 1 thinking is fluid and instinctive, System 2 thinking is the opposite: it's deliberate, conscious, and methodical. System 1 thinking is the proverbial skydiver, where System 2 thinking is the proverbial cautious lawyer. System 2 needs time and labor to process new information—and as a result, it uses more brain energy and can be tiring or draining. That flustered and fatigued feeling you might get while studying or reading a book isn't because you can't understand it or are bored; it's an actual biological imperative. You're using up your System 2 energy.

Both systems of thinking are important to us, as we use them for different situations. Most times, you don't need to stop and think about whether to go at a green light or hug a close friend you haven't seen in a while. They're just things you automatically *do*, and there aren't a lot of considerations or analyses you have to make before you do them. You draw from your past experiences and make an instant decision.

On the other hand, if you're reading a calculus textbook, planning a family budget, or deciding whether to ask someone to marry you, you can't just think casually or rely on your instincts to pull you through. There's a time and place for both System 1 and 2 thinking.

Remember when we said the brain prefers the path of least resistance? This means it favors System 1 thinking whenever possible, and you must force yourself to take a step back and switch into System 2 thinking, which is what we're after most of the time in clear thinking.

System 1 thinking is ultimately quite limiting, which is unfortunate because it's where our minds go first and foremost. It makes us susceptible to accepting things and situations at first glance, not thinking skeptically, being more gullible, and overall faulty thinking. It makes us impulsive and rash without considering consequences or implications. It makes us think *dumber*.

For things you encounter on a regular basis or have deep familiarity with, it's great—this is where System 1 thinking shines. If you have a plethora of experience with a situation, this system can indeed help you make a good decision. It's also obviously useful when dangerous elements are present, as System 1 thinking springs you into action where analysis and careful consideration would leave you dead.

But in situations you're a stranger to (most situations), the instincts of System 1 are almost worthless. System 1 uses familiarity and pre-existing associations to work. Your instincts are based on what you've already known, seen, or experienced; they won't do you any good in a completely unfamiliar situation. You can't go straight from driving a car to operating a sailboat—even though you know how to change direction with a steering wheel, those instincts won't help you when you're trying to change direction with sails.

System 1 also presents certain road bumps in learning. Remember, your brain's preferred default mode is easy (some would say *lazy*). When presented with new material to learn, there's always a chance your brain will take a look at the information and attempt to reduce and simplify all the nuance out of it. Perhaps Kahneman's overall lesson is that we must fight our natural instinct to be lazy thinkers.

But System 2 ain't always what it's cracked up to be either. We can't do it all the time because it would be impractical and too time-consuming. But more importantly, it's plain exhausting, especially if you have to keep forcing yourself to do it. Maintaining your self-control, which is what metacognition is, is an exhausting effort—if you use up all your resources to force yourself to do something, chances are, you'll be less able to do it next time.

This leads to a side effect called *ego depletion*. Expending the mental energy required in System 2 thinking can leave one so drained that it turns their brain into mush and prevents them from exercising it in the near future. If you're pushing yourself to read a chapter of James Joyce's *Ulysses*—not the easiest work of fiction to consume, a

System 2 book if there ever was one—you might not feel up to it next time unless you've formed a System 1-type connection with the material. It'll just be too much. Hand over that cheap romance novel with Fabio's chiseled jawline on the cover.

Ego depletion simply leads to mental fatigue, which doesn't just cause System 1 thinking; it leads to incredibly poor decision-making out of stress, discomfort, and anxiety. After a bruising day at work, it'd be understandable if you decided not to make dinner from scratch—which would probably taste better and be healthier—and just warm up something in the microwave. (On a side note, additional studies on ego depletion have turned up inconclusive results, but we can still make a credible argument that consciously having to think about ten tasks in a day is more mentally strenuous than thinking about two tasks in a day.)

What can we do about this?

First and foremost, attempt to be aware that there are two levels of thinking, and realize that you are probably using System 1 more often than not. Consciously ask yourself if you are making the right choice or merely the quick one. Ask what is driving you—truth or speed. In other words, use metacognition and watch yourself dispassionately and objectively. Draw a contrast between the two types of thinking and become familiar with what each feels like to you. Awareness is the first step to any type of change, because it lets you know where you need to go.

Second, and this is much more difficult, is to transform your System 2 diligence and struggles into System 1 instincts through intentional repetition.

Think of chess masters. For extended periods of time, they have to employ System 2 thinking to understand all the complexities of the game. But after years of experience, they've catalogued thousands of scenarios, effective strategies, and defenses. With all that information *now* at immediate disposal, they can make most of their opening moves without thinking, as all combinations are mere patterns they have seen before, and they only have to switch to System 2 if they run into trouble in the game. Simply put, exposure and consistency shifts us from System 2 to System 1 thinking over time. It eventually becomes the path of least resistance for you.

When you can turn something that requires concentrated effort into something you do habitually, it can be dramatically transformative. The hardest part of any new thing—starting a diet, a new job, learning to drive—always comes at the beginning, when you're using System 2. But after a while, and it's usually not that long, you start to feel more natural in what you're doing, and it becomes a positive habit that you don't have to think too much about (System 1).

If you want chess to be less mentally taxing, it takes time to move all the strategy and combinations from System 2 to System 1.

It's exactly the same way with critical thinking. You are mired in bad thinking habits in System 1. Therefore, begin to intentionally slow yourself down and walk through the steps of analytical and skeptical thinking. It will take time, but it will eventually become a habit, and a habit is really just another way of saying that something has moved from System 2 to System 1 thinking. And eventually it'll be something you just automatically *do*.

Battling Biases

Another way in which we must watch our thinking is in relation to *cognitive biases*. In short, they are additional ways in which the brain instinctively seeks shortcuts and the path of least resistance, which then result in faulty thinking that distorts or misinterprets the truth and could subsequently lead to bad decisions.

A cognitive bias is a pattern of thought that favors one's own experience, beliefs, and subjectivity over reason and objectivity. We all have our own perceptions and opinions about the world and how it works. These beliefs come from our own experience, and we use them to make predictions and judgments about what happens.

The problem with cognitive biases is that they only reflect a single, solitary person's experience: yours. (Or mine.) Your memory of a certain event is colored by your own beliefs about it. And let's face it—that viewpoint is probably biased. Every time a relationship breaks up, each person has their own perception of what went wrong and tends to retell the story of the breakup in ways that make themselves look better and alleviate their fault in the matter. Now imagine this tendency as applied to each and every situation that has open-ended interpretations.

Other times, cognitive biases are a byproduct of downright incorrect thinking and interpretations of the world that, once again, are caused by the brain's proclivity for certainty and System 1 thinking. If we aren't aware that we are operating from a sorely limited worldview and perspective, then we are doomed.

Biases can also come from the two ways in which we organize the limited information we have about the world: *schemas* and *heuristics*. They serve to put what we know about the world into action and facilitate quick decision-making. Each of them goes a long way in producing our psychological triggers.

Schemas. A schema is a model by which we arrange and decipher the information we're currently receiving. It allows us to say, "Okay, based on these three factors I can observe, I know what this is and how to act." Imagine a schema as a snapshot of a certain situation, and we use that snapshot to arrange unfamiliar information.

Introduced by psychologist Jean Piaget, schemas are contextual, and we have schemas for different types of situations. Schemas develop throughout our entire lives, though they're most prevalent when we're learning about something for the first time. But while schemas are extremely useful, they can steer us toward unwarranted biases or errors.

Heuristics. Where schemas help (and hurt) us in learning and interpreting certain things, heuristics are more about how quickly we solve problems and make decisions. A heuristic is a shortcut our minds take when choosing a certain course of action, and as with a schema, it can be helpful or harmful. How do they differ? Where schemas are about understanding a situation at large, heuristics are about your role in a situation and how to act within it. "If this is the situation," a heuristic says, "then I should act in this way."

We make hundreds of decisions every day. Most of them are small, ultimately trivial ones: what we'll have for lunch, what radio station we'll listen to on the way home, what grocery store we're going to shop at, and so forth, unlike major life decisions that could have long-term consequences. We simply can't evaluate every last detail or possible ramification of small decisions. It would be a waste of valuable time and mental energy.

That's where heuristics come in. They're mental guidelines based on past experiences that we use to make basic daily decisions. Think of heuristics as flashcards: they give us quick, abbreviated information to help us make speedy choices about daily decisions that we can't stop and deliberate over.

Like the prior section discusses, our brains are crazy about System 1 thinking and using schemas and heuristics: they take less effort, energy, and time, and make everything simple. Cognitive biases enforce that preference because they encourage snap judgments and quick decisions. As convenient as they are, they blind us to the complex realties that dwell underneath almost everything under the sun.

Cognitive biases do have their uses, however. Sometimes you have to clear the decks of your brain's queue, and to do that, certain *positive* applications of cognitive bias can be good things. But even in those situations, you need to be aware enough to keep your bias from becoming too strong. Having acknowledged this, there are four particular life scenarios where cognitive bias can actually be beneficial:

First. When there's too much information to absorb. We live in a time when there's a deluge of facts, data, statistics, stories, accounts—basically too much information. The overload can be exhausting, and usually contains at least some bits of info that are of no use to us whatsoever. We can become overwhelmed and paralyzed. So it becomes necessary to filter out the information that's relevant and retain only the parts we can use.

Cognitive bias can help reinforce that filter, and it does so in several ways. The brain tends to latch on to the most repeated or recently activated memories (something called the *availability heuristic*, which we'll explain more in a bit). It also tends to remember events or people that are strange or humorous, and notices more strongly when something has changed. So especially when you're in a situation where you experience a lot of repetition—like a day-to-day "grind" job—your brain tends to relate more to what it already knows, as well as when something is odd or different about it.

Of course, when we're experiencing a flood of information, we could fall prey to confirmation bias and deliberately exclude anything that doesn't support our most highly cherished beliefs. And that could mean we're missing out on something extremely important.

Second. When we're struggling to find "meaning" in certain things. We need context for the confusing and varied events that happen in our lives and the things we observe in the world. If we can't derive any meaning or significance from them, we feel adrift and lost. This puts us in an immediate state of vulnerability. To avoid that, we take whatever information we've already filtered and try to find patterns and connections.

Cognitive bias has already reduced the amount of information we have. Now the brain tries to find a certain story in that limited data. In doing so, it relies on our personal experience, looking for past events to compare with this new happening so that it makes some kind of sense to us.

The risk in this, however, is that the brain may rely on outdated stereotypes we have set up or sweeping generalities and judgments we already believe. Also, the brain tends to favor people or things we're comfortable or familiar with—it considers them "better" than people or things we don't like or don't know much about. The brain considers that information too.

In this situation, the cognitive bias won't give a full picture, of course. It's all based on our very limited past experience. But for a moment or two, it's enough for our brains to develop *some* meaning from the situation.

Third. When we need to act quickly. Time puts us into a crunch. Decisions need to be made in fast order. If we let ourselves get bogged down by inactivity or don't react swiftly enough, we can fall behind or risk our survival. Cognitive biases can be helpful in that regard—although, again, not without potential hazards.

Our egos have a role in this action. We have to feel that we're capable of making a positive and important impact. So the cognitive bias may fill us with a sense of confidence (or, more likely, *over*confidence) to get the motor running. In doing this, we may jump to conclusions. But we'll get stuff done and things will be in motion. Sometimes this is indeed the most important factor.

Cognitive biases cause us to fall back on the things that are most familiar and comfortable to us. We rely on the most immediate and available resources. We focus on the present situation, preferring to ponder that instead of the past or the future. We concentrate on things we can more easily relate to and eschew tools or assets that don't make as much sense to us. We strongly prefer solutions that look simple, thorough, and relatively risk-free, rather than answers that are overly complicated, vague, or unsafe.

When the clock's running low, this may be a perfectly reasonable course of action. And it's almost entirely fueled by cognitive bias. But since it comes fast and furious, there might be some cleanup required once everything's settled down.

Fourth. When we're deciding what we need to remember for the future. The final scenario in which cognitive bias might be of assistance concerns memory. If only fragments of our constant information overload are useful to us now, then even less of it will be relevant to us in the days and years to come. So again, we have to cherry-pick the things and details that we remember. Our cognitive bias steps in to shape these memories.

This process basically involves reduction. We'll discard some of the finer specifics of things and events and form broader, more general memories. We trim some of the multiple smaller events off and reshape them into a few basic key points. Maybe we'll pick out only a couple events and elevate them so they represent the whole experience.

In processing these new memories, our cognitive bias again defers to those that are most meaningful or familiar to the brain. It will also "edit" certain memories so they become more accessible to us, but in this process, certain details might accidentally be removed or inserted—so we remember the event slightly differently than how it really happened. And our memory of the experience is more affected by outside circumstances (our condition while the memory was happening, how the information's being presented, and so forth) than by how crucial the information might be.

There are times when cognitive bias can help you, but biases are decidedly not the path to practical intelligence. In fact, they veritably put a blindfold on you. Thus, we must delve into a few of the most prominent biases to understand how to battle them when we can.

Four Cognitive Biases to Watch Out For

Nobody gets by without cognitive biases. They are, by definition, patterns of thought that are undetectable. Cognitive biases lead one to jump to conclusions and make instant rash assessments—and you just can't build a meaningful relationship with practical intelligence if they're all you depend upon. There's reality, and then there's the version of it that your biases create.

In order to use practical intelligence, you must have a firm grasp on reality in its objective form. There are a few specific cognitive biases we'll take a brief look at in hopes that you'll be aware of them and can keep them under control. I'm not going to suggest you *avoid* them, because sometimes they're unavoidable. But I will say they're ones to watch out for—to try to realize when they're happening so you can pause and make at least a brief attempt to think more deeply when they come up. More metacognition.

The availability heuristic. The brain tends to prefer information that's most readily available or comes to awareness rapidly. If something simply comes to mind swiftly or is easily rememberable, we tend to attach an importance to it that it might not really deserve. This heuristic excludes supporting information that might be important to consider, along with countering details that might be used to argue against it.

For example, you might see the topic "tsunamis" trending on Twitter. You follow a couple links to recent "news" reports that say tsunamis are expected to happen more often in the near future. The reports are compelling. You feel a little nervous. You become worried that you'll be a tsunami victim. You start thinking that you haven't prepared enough. You get to the point where you think it's inevitable that someday you'll get swallowed up by a tsunami and there's nothing you can do about it.

In all this concern, you temporarily forget that you live in Kansas, a landlocked state in the middle of the United States where tsunamis never happen. Tsunamis require a large body of water and are best known for happening to small island nations.

That's the availability heuristic in a nutshell: you got spooked by a bunch of instantly accessible information that made you forget the chances of you getting swept away by a tsunami in Kansas are virtually impossible. When you are asked about your fears, you answer "tsunamis" and ignore the rash of home burglaries that might be occurring, or that you are in danger of losing your job. Just because something is available or notable does not mean it is important or representative.

Gambler's fallacy. This common cognitive bias magnifies the importance of past events in the prediction of future outcomes. The bias dictates that conditions and previous results point to the inevitability of something happening down the road— when in reality, each subsequent event is independent of the previous. This bias wants to create a cause-and-effect relationship where none exists. For instance, just because a coin has flipped to the heads side one hundred times in a row doesn't mean it's more likely for the next flip to land on the tails side. There is no relationship between each flip.

This particular cognitive bias is called "gambler's fallacy" because it's responsible for a lot of out-of-control gambling addictions. Somebody betting on a football game may say a certain side will win because they've always done so before, or because they've lost so many times that they are due for a win: "The Packers are due a win this week after all the tough losses, and they are going to get it against the Lions!"

Forget that this guy would be a terrible gambler if that's the information he used to lay a bet, but it illustrates the point. The past history of the Packers-Lions rivalry doesn't have anything to do with how well those teams have played in recent years. The Packers' losses in recent weeks don't mean their turn for a win is coming. *Just because something happened doesn't mean something else will happen.* But someone employing gambler's fallacy would not pay those factors any mind.

Post-purchase rationalization. This cognitive bias seeks to reduce regret, and it's based on a fairly common consumer behavior.

Say you're shopping for home theater equipment. You go to a showroom and see a couple different models. One set of speakers is extremely expensive, features a lot of bells and whistles, and takes up a lot of space. The other's a bit cheaper and smaller, but to the naked ear, doesn't seem to be much different in terms of quality.

You might be persuaded to buy the bigger and more expensive one because, since it's bigger and more expensive, it must work better. But it puts a serious dent in your bank account and is too big for your living room. And you might not even really be able to tell how well the sound's working.

If you employed post-purchase rationalization, you'd convince yourself that you made the right decision, that it's what you wanted to do all along. You'd tell yourself that you can hear the difference in sound, and you do indeed need fifteen different plugs and ports. You might know deep down inside that you went overboard, but that knowledge makes you uneasy. Regret makes you feel stupid, and no one likes that. So you talk yourself into believing you did the right thing and got exactly what you wanted. No more regret, just eating boxed macaroni and cheese for dinner for the next two months because you spent so much on new speakers.

This type of post-*anything* justifying behavior extends far beyond purchases. These are more commonly known as *defense mechanisms*, and they allow us to defend our egos from scrutiny and shame. We do this sometimes when we defend ourselves from others, but here, instead of trying to convince someone else, we are trying to convince ourselves. Sometimes, we are not even aware we are using them. That's the scary part.

Confirmation bias. Confirmation bias is when we want to believe in a certain "fact" so badly that we only look for and agree with information that supports the belief—and ignore compelling evidence that *disproves* it. Instead of "I'll believe it when I see it," confirmation bias dictates a standpoint of "I'll see it when I believe it."

Confirmation bias happens all the time. Those of us with any type of political beliefs tend to consume news from sources that support our opinions and block out legitimate sources that offer countering views. If you are looking to buttress a certain stance that you believe in, you will feel that each supporting source is legitimate and thorough, while each critical source is flawed or has an agenda. There is only one view that you've pre-decided, and you'll mold the evidence to fit it. You see it when you believe it.

Even scientists who supposedly hold objectivity in high esteem might suppress or ignore data that challenges their findings just so they have a better chance of getting published by scientific journals. In fact, this is why an experimental technique called the "double blind" was invented—so scientists didn't know who they were subjecting to certain conditions, and therefore couldn't act in confirmatory ways.

We practice confirmation bias because, quite simply, it hurts to be wrong. Taking the emotional component out of our "truths" as much as possible and being open-minded about divergent views help us combat confirmation bias and think smarter.

Beating Cognitive Bias

So how do we work to defeat cognitive biases that show up in our thinking? The list of four is helpful, but nowhere close to exhaustive. The one thing you can start doing immediately, now that you know what cognitive biases are, is become aware of them in your thinking and interactions and note how they affect your sense of belief. But still, that feels inadequate against some of these thought patterns that have been left unchecked our entire lives.

There are a few specific mental exercises that can help retrain your thinking to become clear-minded and measured.

Practice thinking of alternative explanations. Instead of making a snap decision about why a certain thing is the way it is, try to think of multiple reasons or causes. Reserve your judgment and stop jumping to conclusions. You don't need to find an answer immediately; emphasize the truth instead of speed. For example, if you're sitting in your favorite coffee shop and you notice a huge drop-off in business, you might think it's because the quality of the coffee has declined. But it could also be because more people are making their own espresso drinks, or because it's summer and more people are doing other things outside. Or perhaps it's that the prices the store is charging are keeping people away. (It's usually that, actually.)

In a sense, this is like reverse storytelling. You are starting with the conclusion, but you aren't sure what's happened. Instead of jumping to conclusions, you would work backward and theorize what could have contributed to what you currently see.

You might try an exercise of taking a scene, a person, or any other thing, and observing five details or characteristics about it. Then, for each of those details, write down five possible causes that may have led that particular detail to be the way it is. Try to vary the potential causes you list, ranging from the plainly realistic to the downright bizarre. This will train your ability to create a story around every detail, thus giving you twenty-five trains of thought instead of defaulting to the quickest and easiest for your brain to process.

Most of us think only linearly in terms of cause and effect. But that's ineffective at best in understanding a situation.

Reword your statements as questions. Think of something you consider a declarative, absolute truth. For example: "E-books and e-readers are killing literature." That's a pretty strong statement. But try rephrasing it: "Are e-books and e-readers *really* killing literature?" The mere act of turning it into a question makes your brain start looking for answers: "Well, maybe e-readers are encouraging more people to read—that's good." "They may be changing *how* we read, but they're not really killing how literature is made. Maybe I'm just overly sentimental about physical books." With just that one shift in your statement, you've opened up your mind to a new line of inquiry and exploration.

Get behind and challenge your assumptions. Let's say you have a very broad belief about poor people: "They're poor because they don't want to work." Challenge that assumption immediately: "Do poor people just not want to work? Or do they really have less opportunities? They've been closing plants and stores in town for a few years now—maybe they don't have anywhere else to go. And it's hard to get the proper training for a skilled position when you can't afford it . . . What if there is something else that causes poverty? What if there are about fifty shades of gray to this matter?" The harsh truth is that whatever you think you know about a topic, especially if it involves people's thoughts and motivations, you probably know only about 10 percent of what's truly happening.

It's always best to be proactive about challenging your assumptions through self-interrogation and especially through valid news and information sources—including people who have deep experience in the subject you're thinking of. It's uncertain where many of our assumptions come from anyway, so it's good to reevaluate them from time to time.

Remove pride, ego, and your need to be right. The truth is a separate pursuit entirely from each of those things, and sometimes there is a stark contrast because you want to feel a certain way about yourself, especially in front of others. Truth becomes a lot easier to discern when you take your emotional rewards (and punishments) out of the equation and simply try to determine what's *real*. If you face opposition, it's just going to cause you to dig your heels in and deny, defend, and stonewall. You'll be seduced into caring more about dominating someone than understanding. You'll want to avoid that sour feeling of shame when conceding defeat to someone—anyone. Even if you're right, very few people make friends by saying "I told you so."

Picture how a desperately stubborn person would act—is that similar to how you are acting? Could anyone make an honest comparison between the two? Hopefully not.

Even more so, explore being wrong and understand the feelings that outcome evokes. Play out scenarios where you are indeed wrong. What feelings will you experience? There may be embarrassment, anger, humiliation, or shame—but do they affect the world or your life? Only if you let them.

Logical Arguments

A final element of watching yourself from afar (not dissimilar to a voyeur) is recognizing the naked truth of what's being said. This is deceptively difficult, because just like with cognitive biases, by nature, illogical arguments go unnoticed. It's rare that we dissect statements just to understand their logical underpinnings, and that makes for habitually sloppy arguments and poor understanding. It's easier than you might think, and it is equally frustrating to see people commit these errors on a daily basis.

There's a funny, if somewhat cynical, piece of "advice" for people who are a little unsettled about speaking in public: "If you can't dazzle them with brilliance, baffle them with B.S." In this context, "B.S." does *not* stand for "Bachelor of Science."

We've all been in conversations at least once or twice in our lives in which we realize that the person we're speaking with is making not one shred of sense. They might be talking about a crazy theory they have or speaking from a viewpoint that has no basis in reality. Someone may try to convince you that things are a certain way, but for whatever reason, their words don't add up. It causes a cognitive clog in your brain, and you might end up feeling disoriented or lost.

They probably think they're making sense—they don't *think* they're trying to baffle you with B.S. But on the other hand, maybe they *are*. They might be trying to convolute your thinking with distorted logic and crazy talk.

Whatever the case, you can't quite put your finger on what's wrong, and thus you can't form a rebuttal. That's annoying, to say the least. Someone has gotten the last word on something you're pretty sure is a bad argument, but you can't figure out exactly why.

It's important for you to know that, when these bits of nuttiness are hurled in your direction, it's *not* your brain's fault that you're not getting them. The problem isn't with your comprehension or ability to think—in fact, it's the opposite. You're dealing with someone who is *defying the laws of logic*, and while your ears are taking it all in, your brain's not having any of it. Rightly so.

For the most part, this happens by accident in normal, everyday conversations where people are well-intentioned. People might be so eager to push a stance that they haven't done their due diligence, or someone doesn't pay attention to details and only wants simple sound bites.

We've all done it before. We get caught up in making a firm point, get flustered if we're not convincing enough, and end up making statements that don't seem to make any sense, because they don't. We spitball on earlier statements in an attempt to salvage an argument, and hope they aren't picked apart.

This is a situation where it's beneficial to understand the basic nature of logical thinking and construction. In the world we live in, this understanding is a crucial mental skill to develop. It helps us ferret out the truth and process problems. It imparts the ability to parse arguments and statements and know if they need to be questioned further. In a way, it's a mental model in itself—actually more of a mental *super*model.

Dissecting logical arguments sounds complicated—something you'd need an advanced technical or philosophy degree for—but the foundation of logical thinking is actually pretty easy to understand. The concepts are straightforward. They use sentence structure and equations to illustrate how certain ways of thinking are more effective than others. Understanding them breaks down to assessing the different kinds of statements people make in explaining a concept or an argument.

As a quick example, a friend may be trying to remember their shoe size. They say, "If I am wearing sandals, they will be size nine." So far, so good. And then they say, "Therefore, if I am wearing size nine, I am wearing sandals." Hopefully an alarm has been set off in your brain. That doesn't logically add up, and you're about to learn why.

Conditional statements X -> Y. We'll use a conditional statement as the core example for all these arguments: "If you feed my dog kibbles, then he'll be friendly to you." Just to make things easy to understand, let's pretend in this discussion that this statement is always true.

This is called a conditional statement because it says, "If this condition is met, then this result will 100 percent happen." The condition is your feeding your friend's dog kibbles. The result is that the dog will be friendly to you. There is a straight cause-and-effect relationship between the condition and the result, and it only functions in one direction.

Once again, we're pretending this will always be the case—every time you give this dog a kibble, he's going to love you. Using this as a fact, the statement is sound.

We also call the relationship between the condition and the result one of *premise* and *conclusion*—broader terms that can be used for other statements. If a certain premise is true, then you can expect the conclusion or outcome to be true as well.

These types of statements generally don't present as issues, unless someone is trying to pass off that the conclusion will always be true when it isn't. It's when you start to play with it that problems arise.

Converse statements Y -> X. Now, consider this statement: "If my dog's friendly to you, it's because you fed him kibbles."

Well—that's certainly a *possibility*, since we've determined that feeding the dog kibbles is a surefire way to win his friendliness. But is it the *only* way to make the dog friendly? Maybe you petted him. Perhaps you spoke to him in a gentle, friendly tone of voice. Maybe you played a game of fetch with him that made him extremely happy, and he returned his happiness with affection. Maybe the dog is in a good mood. Dogs do that.

This is an example of a converse statement: it reverses the conclusion and the premise, or the result and the condition—it is saying that the prerequisite is true if the end result is true. And it's turned the statement into a logical flaw. It's true that feeding the dog kibbles will make him your friend. But there's no indication that he's friends with you strictly because you fed him kibbles. There are other ways you can make a dog friendly to you. You've just caught someone. Remember, a statement only has cause and effect in one direction—from condition to result, and not the other way around.

A converse statement is the direct parent of something called the *false syllogism*—basically, a false premise. Its fallacy is also exposed in making leaps of judgment based on misunderstood connections, like this:

- Dogs love kibbles.
- Monkeys love kibbles.
- Therefore, dogs are monkeys.

In this statement, the two premises might be true. But the fact that both dogs and monkeys like kibbles doesn't mean they're the same thing. The premise used for establishing the conclusion—mutual kibble love—is therefore false, as is the conclusion.

Inverse statements Not X -> Not Y. Okay, let's try this one on for size: "If you don't feed my dog kibbles, he won't be friendly to you."

Really? That's the kind of dog you have? If I don't feed him kibbles—if I've run out or, you know, just don't carry kibbles on me out of habit—then he's going to turn on me? What an ingrate.

This is an inverse statement. It preserves the premise-conclusion relationship of the original statement but turns it into a *negative*: "If this doesn't happen, then this won't happen as a result." It assumes a deeper relationship between the two than actually exists. Cause and effect certainly doesn't work if the lack of a cause means the lack of an effect.

Inverse statements are trickier, because not all of them are wrong. Sometimes they're right: "If you don't brush your teeth, then they won't be healthy." Well, that's true. But it leaves out that there are other ways to make your teeth unhealthy. Constantly eating food that's bad for your teeth, for example (even if you do brush).

It could very well be that the dog rejects all who do not bring him kibbles. I don't know this particular dog's neurosis when it comes to being fed kibbles at the appropriate time; I suppose it's possible lack of kibbles turns him into a hostile, nervous wreck.

Still, the dog may be unfriendly for other reasons. Maybe he just got back from chasing a car that he didn't catch, so he's a little disappointed. Maybe he's in a bad mood. Maybe you've insulted him. Maybe he was recently neutered. There are plenty of things that can tick this dog off besides kibble deprivation.

So while certain inverse statements might be right, not all of them will be. Be extra cautious and don't take them at face value. Many things will try to pass themselves off as true statements, but you can begin to see that most of them are logical flaws.

Contrapositive statements Not Y -> Not X. These are statements that negate both the premise and the conclusion—both backward and forward. If the original conditional statement is correct, then the contrapositive is also always true, unlike the converse or inverse statements. This type of relationship does exist both ways, because it's about a negative.

In our trusty dog food analogy, the contrapositive would be "If my dog is unfriendly to you, then you didn't give him kibbles." This is true. There could be many reasons why the dog is being a jerk (see above). But one thing's for sure: if he's unfriendly, then for sure you haven't given him any of his cure-all kibbles. If you did, the dog would be more agreeable. But he isn't, so you haven't. Remember, that part is a given, so if the result is not true, then the given is also not true.

Another quick example: if you go swimming, you will be wet. What might the contrapositive statement sound like? If you are not wet, you did not go swimming. That certainly seems to make sense.

It can take a bit of effort to decipher these types of logical statements, but once you do, you'll find that you can understand the truth of matters instantly.

Takeaways:

- This chapter has a tall task—to get you to think about your thinking. When we're not engaging in what is known as metacognition, it's easy to veer off the path of clear thought. You must become aware of your thought patterns and where you tend to stray. Watch yourself and try to evaluate what's happening inside your brain.

- This process begins with System 1 and 2 thinking, as conceived by Daniel Kahneman. System 1 thinking is quick, instinctual, and decisive—and also often incorrect. System 2 thinking is measured, calm, and analytical—and far slower and more difficult. Unfortunately, the brain operates on the principle of least resistance, so while System 1 thinking is first and foremost, we want to get into the habit of System 2 thinking on a consistent basis. The easier and more familiar a task becomes, the more instinctual and quick it can be, so the way to clearer thinking is consistent repetition and practice.

- Cognitive biases are a similar concept, where we leap to conclusions because they appear to fit schema or heuristics we are familiar with, or are simply in line with our personal experiences. These can also be effective, but often wrong. Notable biases include: availability heuristic (I can remember it, so that means it is important), gambler's fallacy (X happened, which means Y must happen), post-purchase rationalization (I made a good decision . . .), and confirmation bias (I only read what I want to read).

- How can you overcome cognitive biases, aside from simple awareness and metacognition? There are four keys: alternative explanations and reverse storytelling, rewording statements and assumptions as questions, getting behind your implicit assumptions, and removing pride and ego from the equation.

- Finally, it's important to understand logical arguments—and especially illogical arguments. We hear these every day but may not be able to pick out their logical flaws. You can think of these as a combination of math and argumentation that allows us to see the reality versus what you see or hear. There is the conditional statement (X -> Y, true), the converse statement (Y -> X, usually a flaw), the inverse statement (Not X -> Not Y, usually a flaw), and the contrapositive statement (Not Y -> Not X, true). It's not just word games; it's understanding the foundations upon which real and false arguments are built.

Chapter 3. Think in Models

At this point, we've examined how our brains work on a biological level to periodically sabotage us. We'll go along with the theme of being more intentional about our thinking as we introduce the concept of *mental models* and how they can act as a virtual safeguard against unintelligent (stupid) thinking.

The name Charlie Munger might not ring a bell. You're probably more familiar with his business partner, Omaha billionaire Warren Buffett, one of the world's most famous investors. The two of them have worked side by side for Buffett's multi-conglomerate Berkshire Hathaway since 1978. Although Munger isn't in the spotlight as much as his partner, Buffett credits an overwhelming amount of his success to their alliance.

Munger emerged from the shadows to give a commencement speech at USC Business School in 1994 entitled "Lesson on Elementary, Worldly Wisdom as It Relates to Investment Management & Business." The impact of Munger's speech has proven to be highly influential in the decades after it was delivered, as it introduced the concept of "mental models," which was subsequently disseminated to the public at large. He mused,

> "What is elementary, worldly wisdom? Well, the first rule is that you can't really know anything if you just remember isolated facts and try and bang 'em back. If the facts don't hang together on a latticework of theory, you don't have them in a usable form. You've got to have models in your head. And you've got to array your

experience—both vicarious and direct—on this latticework of models.

You may have noticed students who just try to remember and pound back what is remembered. Well, they fail in school and in life. You've got to hang experience on a latticework of models in your head.

What are the models? Well, the first rule is that you've got to have multiple models—because if you just have one or two that you're using, the nature of human psychology is such that you'll torture reality so that it fits your models, or at least, you'll think it does. You become the equivalent of a chiropractor who, of course, is the great boob in medicine.

It's like the old saying, 'To the man with only a hammer, every problem looks like a nail.' And of course, that's the way the chiropractor goes about practicing medicine. But that's a perfectly disastrous way to think and a perfectly disastrous way to operate in the world.

So you've got to have multiple models. And the models have to come from multiple disciplines—because all the wisdom of the world is not to be found in one little academic department. That's why poetry professors, by and large, are so unwise in a worldly sense. They don't have enough models in their heads. So you've got to have models across a fair array of disciplines.

You may say, 'My God, this is already getting way too tough.' But, fortunately, it isn't that tough—because eighty or ninety important models will carry about ninety percent of the freight in making you a worldly-wise person. And of those, only a mere handful really carry very heavy freight."

Additionally, Munger asserted the following about mental models: "You must know the big ideas in the big disciplines and use them routinely—all of them, not just a few. Most people are trained in one model—economics, for example—and try to solve all problems in one way.

Munger makes it clear that to navigate the world without a well-rounded set of mental models is tantamount to taking stabs in the dark. There are too many variables for one to deal with effectively, and unless you have a model for which to organize them, things will go poorly. If life is a construction site, mental models would be how to use a hammer, a saw, nails, a sander, and so on. The more models you acquire, the better you can deal with the job.

So then what exactly is a mental model? It's a filter of sorts to run situations through to try to quickly gain understanding and make an optimal decision. They provide guidance to us as sort of rules of thumb for living. You can call them life heuristics or guidelines to evaluate and comprehend. You can also think of them as a set of goggles you can strap on that will help you pay attention to certain elements and think toward a specific goal.

They give us the ability to filter noise from the signal. No model is an entirely perfect reflection of the world, but they don't have to be. As long as they help us evaluate the complexity around us, they can be used to improve our decisions. Skepticism and critical thinking are essentially mental models for specific purposes. If our purpose is practical intelligence, we can easily adjust for that as well.

We already have our own mental models; they're what we've developed over the course of our lives. Every one of us possesses a set of values, ideas, and processes that we apply to what we see going on around us. Based on our own experiences, we've learned to process conditions and solve problems in a certain way. You may refuse to use banks out of distrust for large institutions and keep your money tucked under your mattress as a rule of thumb. While self-reliance and eschewing large institutions can be seen as a mental model, it may not be very effective, smart, or even applicable to most areas of life.

By definition, our own mental models are limited and only reflect a biased perspective. These are the proverbial hammers Munger speaks of—our limited views.

If *my* mental approach is the *only* thing I use when I'm trying to perceive and understand the world, I'm not going to have a very broad spectrum of comprehension about the world. Invariably, I will get some things completely wrong, and will come up blank in other situations when nothing in my experience can apply.

Therefore, the more, the better. Understanding a certain object, action, event, or subject through a new viewpoint or set of standards helps you discover multiple facets about what you see, and could offer a wider array of potential solutions than you'd have if you stuck to your own frame of reference.

This is especially helpful if these models are universal, widely applicable, and tend to lead to answers and truth rather than speculation and opinion. The more varied perspectives you possess, the more you can view the world in terms you can understand. *It's truly not what you know, but how you think.*

For example, take *the Pareto Principle*, a mental model that's a personal favorite. It's also called the *80/20 Rule*. It states that in any given endeavor, 80 percent of the effects are caused by 20 percent of the causes. When you're in a scenario where you're trying to determine efficiency and what to focus on, you can strap on your Pareto Principle goggles. You can use this mental model to find that in the office, 80 percent of sales come from 20 percent of the customers; in a doctor's office, 80 percent of all sports injuries are caused by the most common 20 percent of the hazards; in the gym, 80 percent of the weight lost is caused by 20 percent of the exercises, and so on. Now, the model might not hold true, and the numbers certainly won't always be so exact, but it gives you an idea of how to organize your information and decision-making without even having to know anything beforehand.

It's a general rule of thumb that can produce a helpful truth about trends, possibilities, decisions, and insights we wouldn't have otherwise. It's a useful hammer for a certain type of situation.

You can see how it benefits you to have a wide range of mental models to employ. As useful as the Pareto Principle is, it doesn't help you decide where to go on vacation, for instance. You could try (80 percent of the enjoyment of a vacation comes from 20 percent of the factors), but it's not quite suited for it.

Of course, that's also what Munger espoused in his reference to a *latticework* of mental models. You need multiple models from a wide variety of disciplines because life has innumerable dimensions. In fact, the power of mental models lies in having a latticework that is applicable across many situations.

If you don't have this framework, you risk falling prey to the fable of the blind men and the elephant, which goes something like the following: there were once six blind men, and they all reached out and could only feel different parts of an elephant: the knee, the side, the tusk, the trunk, the ear, and the tail. They all came to the conclusion that they were feeling different animals or objects. None of these blind men were wrong in isolation, but they could only see from a single perspective, so they were wrong about the elephant's overall appearance. In other words, not everything is solvable using the Pareto Principle.

Multiple models challenge each other to produce a more unified overview, whereas just using one or two restricts your long-range view to a limited context or discipline. Having a huge range of mental models can expand your viewpoint and cancel out some of the stray "errors" that using just one or two models would produce.

This doesn't mean you have to know all the ins and outs of a million different disciplines to employ multiple mental models. You just need to understand the basic points and fundamentals of a few essential ones. Just don't be the person with a single hammer.

Models in Brief

Munger didn't go into specifics about his own latticework of mental models he used to make decisions. That's because his particular set of models wouldn't necessarily work for anyone else but him. He provided some tips to *identify* what models you might want to consider, but he didn't lead anyone down the path himself. That's a journey only you can make.

But for the sake of explanation, here are a few examples of mental models so you have an idea of what they look like and how to break them down:

Think about secondary consequences. When you're considering making a certain decision, think about the consequences the decision would have down the line— second, or third order outcomes, and further down the line if you can. If you are going to tip over a domino, think about the second and third dominoes to fall. They might not be the ones you intend. It's easy to imagine how a course of action is going to affect the immediate situation, but only focusing on fixing the problem at hand could result in other problems arising.

So to choose the most appropriate solution, think of what will happen down the road should you elect to put it into effect. In other words, think longer-term and outside your immediate circle of concern. When you run situations through this mental model, you'll find answers that are more beneficial overall rather than engaging in immediate gratification.

Satisficing. This word was introduced in 1956 as a combination of the words "satisfy" and "suffice." The idea behind the mental model of satisficing is that in some situations, a perfect or optimal solution is impossible—no reasonable solution will fix every single problem that could use attention, and an "optimal" solution is either impossible or impractical.

You will simply waste time and energy searching for something that either doesn't exist or doesn't really make a difference. Do you need *optimal* peanut butter, or will most of them do? If you can take a step back and understand that you only need to achieve the goal of buying peanut butter, you can move on with your life. What appears to be "best" is largely subjective and nothing you will probably ever notice.

In satisficing, one retrains their focus on the most important or pivotal points that need to be addressed (not unlike the Pareto Principle), and then makes decisions that will satisfice in that context. Trying to come up with an exact and precise answer every single time is a needless waste of time and energy. When you run situations through this mental model, you'll understand what your actual purpose is, what's secondary, and what you can ignore completely.

Distinguish feeling or thinking. It's easy to mistake emotions for thoughts. Both deal with a sense of conviction. But emotions are immediate responses to certain sensory stimuli that aren't always controllable, whereas thoughts come from a standpoint of calculation and consideration. This harkens back to the discussion of System 1 and System 2 thinking.

In the feeling-vs.-thinking mental model, you try to instill an objective point of view as much as you can. This means removing your emotional investment about a certain circumstance or problem and surveying the evidence as a disinterested outsider. You might even try some reverse emotional engineering for a problem and consider how you might deal with a situation if you *wanted* to be emotional about it. Then you'd compare and contrast it with the situation you're dealing with at the moment. Hopefully they are radically different plans of attack.

The point of this model is to reduce the chance that you'll make an errant decision based solely on instinct, impatience, or temper. It's also a way to make sure you're not confusing emotions with intellectual reasoning, and to help you gain some clarity on the inherent differences between the two. Emotional thinking can occasionally be important and even necessary, but for important decisions, clear thinking should always be the primary consideration. When you run situations through this mental model, you will understand what emotional attachments you have that are holding you back.

Prioritize motion. Many of us have a tendency to plan a course of action across every step, accounting for every potential smaller action along the way and coming up with contingencies if something doesn't go right. While *some* planning is a good idea, too much planning can delay the decision from being executed. In worst-case scenarios, spending most of the time in prep mode can result in what's commonly called "analysis paralysis"—getting mired in the planning stage so much that nothing ever gets done.

This mental model encourages you to start with doing and stop standing still. Stop trying to reason in your head, and put pen to paper. Whatever it is, take a step beyond your instinct.

Make your default course of action actual, not just more planning. You don't need to know every single step along the way and have a detailed set of instructions ready to go. You just need to be able to anticipate the next step or two. If you set off on a road trip, you don't need the exact address you are driving to—you just need enough directions for the next hour or two.

Part of the problem is hesitation from not feeling prepared. But the truth is, you'll never be 100 percent prepared, not close to it. You'll learn more and become more prepared by taking a single step forward and learning through experience versus endless planning from the sidelines. No matter how hard you plan, things will come up that you couldn't have planned for, and your end destination might even change in the process. Mistakes? Ninety-nine percent are reversible or inconsequential.

If it feels too early to start a certain task, that might be a sign that it's the *perfect* moment to get going. When you run situations through this mental model, you will be quicker and farther along than anyone else.

Whatever can go wrong will go wrong. You might recognize this mental model as Murphy's Law. Sometimes it is used in jest to lament someone's misfortunes, but it can be far more useful than as a joke.

You can use this principle when you decide on the readiness of something, or whether you yourself are prepared. If there is a possibility that it can go wrong, you had better fix it. If you know there is a weak spot, you had better address it. The point of this model is to use uncertainty as a sign for action. You'll look differently at your decisions if you think that any chink in the armor can lead to disaster.

When you run situations through this mental model, you will find yourself weighing the costs and benefits of allowing a mistake.

Of course, this might come into odds with the prior mental model of prioritizing action, but that's precisely where having a latticework is helpful. Not all motion is helpful, and not all double-checking is helpful, but the models give you two concrete options for how to deal with something.

These five models can work together and cover a wide variety of situations to help you navigate life. But more specifically to our goal of practical intelligence and understanding the world for what it is, we'll explore three additional mental models in greater depth.

Process Versus Outcome

Sometimes, we get obsessed with outcomes. It makes sense. We work really hard to achieve them. They're our goals; we think about the moment of victory when we are trudging along in the trenches.

If outcomes influence our decision processes, it means that we are heavily blinded by *outcome bias*.

Outcome bias means that you repeat a process, solution, or decision because the outcome was positive instead of thinking through the steps that led to that outcome. In other words, you are saying, "Well, I don't know why, but that solution worked last time. So let's do it again!" But if that's all the thought you give it, you're relying more on luck than anything else.

Focusing on the outcome means that you are simply working with incomplete information. *What do X and Y matter if you attain the outcome you want?* This type of thinking can easily bleed over into a mental habit of ignoring critical thinking and reinforcing bad thought patterns. We give outcomes too much power; we don't want to be fooled by the proverbial stopped clock, which is correct twice a day.

Here's a clear example to understand outcome bias. Imagine that you went out to a bar and had a few drinks. One of your best friends showed up and you stayed out even later and drank way more than you had expected. But you still drove home, even though you were drunk. You arrived at home without any incident. In this case, the outcome is good. Great, even! You got home safely, and you didn't even have to spend money on a taxi. But that doesn't mean the decision to drive drunk was a good idea. If you were swayed by outcome bias, you might think that driving drunk was no big deal because it had worked out in the past.

Most people are able to recognize that the decision to drive drunk was bad and the outcome was good. Thus, bad decisions can sometimes lead to good outcomes. Good decisions can also lead to bad outcomes.

But the only thing we can do is the best with what we have at the moment, and that means we have to evaluate and analyze the decisions, not the outcomes.

It turns out that outcome bias is pervasive. In the world of poker, it even has a special name: *resulting,* in which competitors focus only on the results of a game. In poker, players' decision-making can become easily muddled by what worked well the last time they played. However, the best way to play is by thinking about what is most likely to occur and making decisions based on probabilities. The outcomes in the past can play a small role but are only a single factor among many others.

World-renowned poker player and author Annie Duke once encountered outcome bias when she attended a charity poker tournament. Looking at a sneak peek of the players' cards, she told the crowd that player A's cards had a 76 percent chance of winning, while player B's cards had a 24 percent chance of winning. Player B won.

A member of the audience shouted that she had made a mistake. But just because it was more likely that player A would win didn't mean it would happen. Betting on player A's hand was a better decision to make with the information the bettor had when they first saw the cards, even though it wasn't guaranteed. If Duke were to then use outcome bias, she might bet on a player with player B's cards in the future, even though it's not the best hand because on this one occasion, that hand won.

In your office or workplace, outcome bias may also take place. For example, your boss hires a new employee through your obsolete and outdated hiring process of a single written test. Then, instead of evaluating the hiring process to see if it was thoughtful or fair, your boss only focuses on the new hire's performance and whether or not they've achieved good outcomes. Suppose they do earn the company a lot of money. The company sees no need to change what is already working or to "fix what ain't broke."

More than likely, this means that the company's ancient hiring processes remain terrible and that the company is extremely susceptible in the future to terrible hires. If it goes unchecked, the interview process may cost the company money when poor hiring decisions are made over and over again. For instance, the next employee the company hires immediately begins embezzling money and then flees to Mexico with a seven-figure payout. This could have been prevented by simply trying to ensure a better decision process.

Notably, you have to be careful not to confuse outcome bias with *hindsight bias*. With hindsight bias, the correct choice seems obvious thanks to being able to see how things played out. However, the answer may not have been clear at the time the decision or choice was made. For example, you might say, "I knew it was going to rain" as it starts to rain. But it had been sunny earlier in the day and you hadn't watched the weather report, so there's no way you could have known it was going to rain. This differs from outcome bias, in which case you might decide to always carry an umbrella.

So how can you avoid the negative effects of outcome bias and create a better decision process? What can you do to avoid getting caught in this trap?

Evaluate the decision-making process *before* outcomes have been achieved. Consider this example. There are two doctors. One of the doctors offered a patient a cheaper medicine with great results in studies. The other doctor offered their patient a more expensive medicine for which they also earned a commission, and this medicine also had similarly great results.

Right now, ask yourself which doctor you think made the best decision. You'd probably view the first doctor in a more positive light than the second one. After all, the first doctor appears to have the patient's best interests in mind while the second doctor is concerned with enriching himself.

As for outcomes? It turns out that the patient of the first doctor suffered from a side effect of the medicine and had to be hospitalized for a day. The other patient didn't suffer any side effects and recovered fully. Does your opinion on the decision change at all? It shouldn't, though there is a natural tendency to switch sides. Indeed, in a study, respondents who knew about the outcomes exhibited outcome bias by viewing the second doctor more positively when compared to the first.

The outcome can skew your perspective and make you less likely to appreciate how the first doctor had the patient's best interests in mind, while the second doctor acted selfishly. Instead, you focus on the bad outcome, in which the first patient suffered and blamed it on his doctor, even if either medicine had an equal chance of causing a side effect.

In other words, learning an outcome can change how you view behaviors and intentions. To make sure you value intentions and the decision-making process, do this evaluation before you know the outcome. Or wait until after you've completed your evaluation to learn the outcome.

Along the same lines, make an explicit effort to think about what people want to accomplish (their intentions) rather than the outcome. However, Francesca Gino, an expert at Harvard Business School, says that even this strategy of highlighting intentions can't always help people avoid outcome bias. The best bet, she says, is not taking outcomes into account at all when making decisions.

If you're evaluating candidates for a promotion, start by considering factors that don't have to do with outcomes. Is this employee hard-working? Do they arrive on time? Are they a good communicator? Do they contribute meaningful ideas? Are they making a good effort and doing what they are supposed to be doing?

These are all things employees can control; they cannot control outcomes. If we were to only go on outcomes, we would be evaluating these candidates based on how lucky they were. And that's not the basis for sound decisions.

This mental model as a policy is best phrased as "if you build it, they will come," where "it" is the decision process and "they" is the result you are seeking.

Storytell in Reverse

For those of us who are more artistically inclined, this is your moment to shine.

A *fishbone diagram* is a method that allows you to identify multiple potential causes for a problem or an effect. Being able to infer causes based on an observed effect is an integral aspect of deduction, especially when it comes to problem-solving. Fleshing out a list of all the possible causes of a problem simultaneously provides you with a blueprint of the specific factors you need to focus on to ultimately find viable solutions.

The fishbone diagram is so structured that those causes are placed in categories, so you get a more orderly perspective of the entire situation. It's a more organized way of working in reverse from effect to cause and is a frequently used tool for structuring brainstorming sessions. The end product is a visual display of all the factors—both from a micro and a macro perspective—that play a role in the effect or the problem.

To make a fishbone diagram, first write a problem statement or effect somewhere in the middle right portion of a whiteboard or any writing surface you've chosen. Draw a box around it, then a horizontal line across the page that ends in that problem box. That box will serve as the "head" of the fishbone.

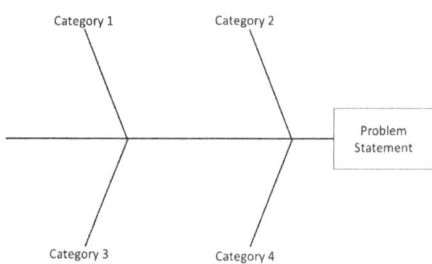

Next, draw the "bones" of the body by sketching widely spaced vertical lines that extend from the main horizontal line. Draw bones above and below the main line, slightly slanting away from the head of the fishbone. These bones will be labeled with the different categories of the causes you come up with. It's up to you to name the categories that apply to the problem you're working on.

Every time you come up with a possible cause for the problem, write it down as a connection to the particular "bone" it's categorized under. You can write the same cause under multiple categories, if applicable. Then, for each noted cause, continue asking what might've caused it and write it down as a connection to that cause—and so on until you can no longer think of a more primary cause. This will allow you to exercise your deductive reasoning skills until you arrive at the most fundamental root causes of the problem.

When you're done with the diagram, scrutinize the causes you've listed and consider the evidence. How much does the identified cause really contribute to creating the effect? Is its link with the problem well-established and significant enough to consider seriously? Get into the habit of thinking, "What would make this cause a true and significant factor in the problem at hand?"

For example, say you're a hotel manager trying to understand the causes of low customer satisfaction ratings for your hotel service. Write the problem in a box as the fishbone "head" and the categories of possible causes (in this case, the four Ps of service industries) as the main "bones." Doing this, the initial stages of your fishbone diagram would look like so:

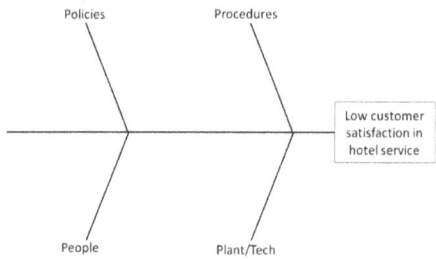

Then start filling in each category with possible causes. For example, you've identified that possible causes for the problem are (1) the slow resolution of customer complaints and (2) the hotel staff's inability to be sensitive to the customers' needs, thus leading the customer to become dissatisfied with the service.

Asking yourself why your staff may lack sensitivity to customer needs, you may consider that they work such long hours that they are reduced to providing the bare minimum of service; they no longer have enough energy to pay more attention to customers' specific needs. Given that, your fishbone diagram would now indicate the following:

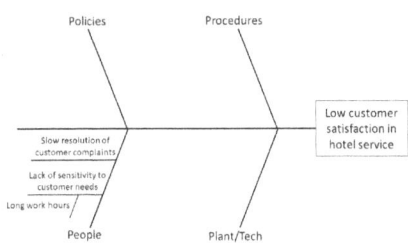

Continuing the process of asking yourself why the problem exists, you start identifying more possible causes and noting them under the given categories, leading your diagram to look something like this:

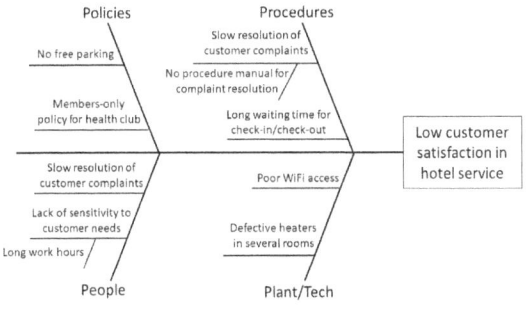

By systematically working backward from the problem to the causes, you get to identify specific aspects of your situation that you can then address accordingly. The fishbone diagram is a tool that effectively focuses your efforts to solve the problem at its roots—or, in this case, at its bones.

It's a great way to guide your thinking in the process of reverse storytelling, as it allows you to concretely trace how the problem is linked back to specific causative factors.

Try watching a scene, a person, or any other thing and observing ten details about it. Then, for each of those specifics, write down five possible causes that may have led that particular detail to be the way it is. Try to vary the potential causes you list, ranging from the plainly realistic to the downright bizarre. This will train your ability to create a story around every detail and consider what preceded it, thus exercising your skills in reverse storytelling.

Separate Correlation from Causation

In efforts to understand why certain events happen, we must go looking for instigating factors. It's only logical that we try to find a previous event directly responsible for *causing* the event we're looking at. This is what we should spend our time trying to fix, but it turns out that we might be spending all of our energy on the wrong issue. We're fooled into confusing correlation for causation. One of this mental model's shining examples follows.

Say you're looking at a graph that depicts two data comparisons—one axis shows the total number of sunglasses sold over a period of time, and the other shows the total sales of ice cream. During the summer months, you note that sales of both items increase and that they tend to go down after summer is over.

Looking at this graph, you might come to the conclusion that sales of ice cream directly impact sales of sunglasses. People are buying more sunglasses because they're buying more ice cream—or the other way around. No matter the direction, it appears that one is causing the other.

Why might this be the case? Is it because there are stores that sell both ice cream *and* sunglasses? Is there something about buying a sundae or root beer float that triggers one to grab a pair of Ray-Bans immediately after? Do sunglasses press on a facial nerve that triggers sugar cravings?

These theories sound ridiculous, don't they? That's because they are.

When you first read the example, you probably figured out that sales of ice cream and sunglasses increased due to the arrival of summer. Since there are more hot and sunny days in summer, people are more inclined to buy cold treats like ice cream and protective eyewear like sunglasses. People don't buy sunglasses as a direct result of ice cream purchases—they buy both when the summer heat hits them. Just because two things occur simultaneously doesn't mean there is a causal relationship *between* them.

Even though that's a pretty broad example, it reflects a logical error that lots of people make—sometimes about matters even *more* elementary and basic than ice cream and sunglasses. That error is believing that since two events have similar patterns or related behaviors, one must be causing the other to happen. This is the mistake of believing that *correlation implies causation*. In fact, they are entirely separate concepts.

Correlation is a statistical term. It shows that two individual elements or variables share similar traits or trends—"ice cream and sunglasses sales both *increased*." That's all there is to correlation: two things behave similarly in this way or that way. Correlation does *not* describe why or how the relationship between two items is the way it is; it doesn't give a reason. It just says, "These two things are generally doing the same thing at the same time."

Causation, on the other hand, is an effort to establish the reason things happen—also referred to as "cause and effect." The message of causation is: "This thing changed, which in turn *caused* this other thing to change." In our super-basic example, the thing that actually caused the increase in sunglasses revenue was the arrival of summer, which was also responsible for the boost in ice cream sales. There was a causal relationship between summer and sunglasses and summer and ice cream, but there's only a correlative relationship between sunglasses and ice cream.

To believe that the increase in ice cream sales *caused* the rise in sunglasses sales is a logical mistake. This is countered by the phrase *correlation doesn't imply causation*—just because two events are similar doesn't mean one is causing the other one to happen. There may be another underlying factor that's causing *both* things to happen.

This error in thinking usually happens when there's a lack of information at our disposal—or, perhaps more frequently, when we don't take the time to observe all the information we should. Jumping to conclusions is always a temptation when we feel under pressure to come up with a definitive answer. In order to avoid that fallacy, one should identify as many potential factors as one can: research, study trends, gather more data, and make reasonable, unhurried judgments.

In a lot of cases, correlations are nothing more than flukes or chance, yet we rapidly jump to causal conclusions. When evaluating cause and effect, the default mental model should always be to separate correlation from causation and not assume a causal relationship unless you can definitively say so.

There's one more wrinkle when it comes to discussing cause and effect. It's a bit more complex than we're led to believe as children, when we're taught that pushing on a toy truck will make it move.

As we gain more life experience, causal factors become a little more complicated. There are more conditions, underlying motives, and elements that affect events. Sometimes it's hard to point to a singular cause, because it's hard to say that element acted alone or wasn't the product of multiple mini-causes.

This process involves looking past the immediate reason things happen (the *proximate* cause) and searching for a greater, more fundamental basis that makes things happen (the *root* cause). The proximate cause is to the root cause as correlation is to plain causation. Solving for the former (proximate cause; correlation) won't rid you of your troubles.

For example, say somebody's driver's license gets suspended. Let's call him Hal. Traffic court has been waiting for Hal to respond to a series of speeding violations, but he's never complied. A warrant for Hal's arrest is issued; the police go over to his home, bust down his door, and throw him in jail for a long weekend.

At this point, we can ask the question, why is Hal in jail? Well, he's there because police were acting on an arrest warrant that said he needed to answer for multiple speeding violations. This is the *proximate* cause: the most recent, basic actions that led to Hal being thrown into the slammer.

But the proximate cause doesn't explain the deeper issues that have led to Hal's being in jail. You could say the arrest warrant was issued because Hal's a lead-foot who needs to lighten up on the accelerator pedal. So you could consider Hal's need for speed to be the *root* cause.

But is it?

One can keep going down a rabbit hole to find out *why* Hal is this way, and you could continue to consider each new level a *more* root cause. If he's going to change his ways, simply telling him to stop speeding so much might not be effective. What's causing him to speed? Maybe his parents never taught him restraint in certain situations; they just let him dart around the house and make a mess of things, and that recklessness followed him into adulthood. At this point, Hal has a *deeper* root cause—some have called this level arriving at the *ultimate* cause. Unless Hal deals with the emotional basis for his speeding habit, there's a great chance he'll re-offend. If he blows off the charges and just blames "the man," he hasn't learned anything.

This is the proximate/root cause portion of this mental model in a nutshell. It's a more critical and profound way of discovering the *real* answers and explanations for events. Quality thinking means going past the proximate cause—which is usually just a physical sequence of cues—and understanding the factors, thinking or emotional patterns, or environmental elements that set the groundwork for what has taken place.

It might help to imagine each set of actions as motivated by something psychological. One way of putting this discovery plan into action is the "five whys" method, which is simply asking "why" five times to establish a deeper root cause:

Why is Hal in jail? Because there was an arrest warrant out for him (proximate cause).

Why? Because he hadn't responded in court to his multiple speeding violations.

Why? Because he exceeded the speed limit nine times and got caught.

Why? Because he has a "need" or impulse to go super-fast on the highway.

Why? Because he never had a set of boundaries as a child and thought he could do whatever he wanted without consequences.

Differentiating between proximate and root causes makes one keep going in the discovery process—whereas, left to one's own instincts, a person might stop asking once they identify the immediate cause or even when they see a vague correlation. By going deeper, you'll get a better understanding of why things happen and be better positioned to deal with problems.

Takeaways:

- One of the best ways to embody practical intelligence is Charlie Munger's concept of mental models. These are heuristics, or handy rules of thumb, for how to approach situations in smart ways. It's when we try to freelance everything in our lives that we truly run into trouble, so having (relatively) universal guidelines or blueprints for how to act intelligently and efficiently can be invaluable.

- Among the innumerable approaches that exist, we talk about the Pareto Principle (80/20 ratio), thinking about secondary consequences, distinguishing between feeling and thinking, satisficing (satisfy + suffice), prioritizing motion over planning, and addressing Murphy's Law (whatever can go wrong, will go wrong).

- Three mental models are specifically suited toward our purpose of practical intelligence and acting within the bounds of common sense. First, we discuss the difference between evaluating a process versus an outcome. Often we can fall into the trap of outcome bias, wherein we ignore our decision process simply because something turned out favorably. Second, we learn to tell stories in reverse using the fishbone diagram analysis. This is a powerful tool to deal with the problem of cause and effect and illuminate our thinking to the possibilities of alternative perspectives. Third, we come to separating correlation from causation, and understanding the true relationships between events we observe.

Chapter 4: Thought Divergence

Once upon a time, there was a widget company who was negotiating with a real-estate company for a lease. The widget company wanted to lease an office for below the listed price—in fact, substantially below. The real-estate company's owner took offense to this, and the two parties engaged in a series of passive-aggressive e-mails until it finally boiled over into direct aggression. This quickly escalated into a shouting match at the real-estate company office, which included statements such as, "You're all about the money, aren't you?" and, "You're so greedy, I should call you Scrooge!"

Ignoring the fact that both of these businesses are indeed businesses with the main purpose of generating revenue, this negotiation could have been easily managed by taking a step back and utilizing *divergent thinking*. This is practical intelligence with regards to problem solving and making something out of what's placed in front of you. We can't always control what we end up with, but we still must find a way to accomplish our goals.

Instead of arguing about only one element—the rent itself—the parties could have rephrased the transaction to focus on themselves: "If I am not getting the rent I want, what else is on the table?" For the real-estate company, this would consist of asking what they could want from the widget company that would make up for the decrease in revenue. For the widget company, this would consist of asking what they could provide to the real-estate company to justify a lesser rent.

The parties might come to a compromise where in exchange for the lesser rent, the widget company takes over trash and recycling duties for the entire building, or they allow the real-estate company to also work out of their office every week. Instead of continually banging heads over the same resource, a win-win situation would be found.

Now, rarely are negotiations so easily solvable, but the point is there would never even be an opportunity to come to a satisfactory compromise if divergent thinking wasn't used.

For our purposes, you can think of divergent thinking as the precursor to creative thinking, and you'll find that they are typically defined similarly. Divergent thinking is usually defined as thinking and opening your mind in different directions, similar to how water ripples outward from a central point. Someone using divergent thinking is actively eschewing the existing options and looking for alternative ones, or to create their own.

The contrast to this is *convergent thinking*, which is when thoughts come together and coalesce in only a few options. Someone using convergent thinking is focused on finding cracks or openings in what's already in front of them, and isn't interested in exploring or thinking creatively. You can imagine convergent thinking to be a focused beam of light, illuminating only two doors, where divergent thinking is a more scattered and unfocused beam, dimly illuminating five doors. The easiest illustration for this is the simple act of brainstorming—coming up with as many ideas as possible on a certain topic or how to address a problem.

Thus, divergent thinking reflects what we require most often in the real world. Rarely will we enjoy the luxury that our options are laid out neatly in front of us, and all we have to do is compare and contrast. No, practical intelligence requires that you seek out and seize solutions—the deeper the insight, the less accessible it is, after all.

These two approaches can work together—start the creative thinking process with divergent thinking, and then evaluate your options with convergent thinking. But most of us start this process at the end, without using our creativity to create the necessary insights. This is the last piece to practical intelligence—how to think outside the box and marry creative thinking with analytical and critical thinking.

SCAMPER Method

One of the easiest ways to cultivate out-of-the-box thinking is the SCAMPER method. Pioneered by Bob Eberle to spark creativity during brainstorming sessions, the SCAMPER method stands for seven techniques that help direct thinking toward innovative ideas and solutions: (S) substitute, (C) combine, (A) adapt, (M) minimize/magnify, (P) put to another use, (E) eliminate, and (R) reverse. Collectively, these techniques are based on the idea that you can come up with something new by simply modifying the old elements already present around you.

The SCAMPER method works by forcing your mind to think in a new, specific flow, making it possible for you to reach novel solutions. Think of it as akin to opening a faucet that introduces water to seven pipes, and each of those pipes channels to a unique pot of earth. Each pot has the potential to bring forth a new growth once the seeds in it are watered. The SCAMPER method works in a similar way to nurture a new idea or solution out of you.

Note that the SCAMPER method doesn't require that you move in a sequential flow of steps. You may start with any of the thinking techniques it involves and jump among the different methods throughout your brainstorming or problem-solving session. Furthermore, it adapts the principle of *force-fitting*. This means that in order to come up with fresh solutions, you should be willing to integrate ideas, objects, or elements together—no matter how dissimilar, unrelated, or apparently illogical they seem to be. Those perceptions are mental boundaries that are holding you back.

Only by freeing your mind enough to connect things you never thought of linking before can you fully harness each of the following thinking techniques of the SCAMPER method. Indeed, this is a major element of SCAMPER because we are too often held back by our preconceptions and assumptions of what cannot be.

Substitute. This technique refers to replacing certain parts in the product, process, or service with another to solve a problem. To carry out this technique, first consider the situation or problem in light of having many elements—multiple materials, several steps in the process, different times or places at which the process can occur, various markets for the product or service, and the like. Then consider that each and every one of these elements may be replaced with an alternative.

Some questions that might help you get into this flow of thinking include the following: "Could a more cost-effective material replace the current one we're using without sacrificing product quality?" "What part of the process can be switched into a simpler alternative?" "In what other places can we offer our services?"

Let's say you're involved in the production of craft pieces that use a particular kind of glue as adhesive. However, you find that the glue you use easily dries out and clumps up even when stored properly, leading to wastage and higher production costs. To solve this problem, consider brainstorming whether you might find a different adhesive to replace what you're currently using. Another example might be substituting local materials for imported ones, not only reducing costs on your end but also helping the local community in the process.

Combine. This technique suggests considering whether two products, ideas, or steps of a procedure may be combined to produce a single output or process that's better in some way. Two existing products could create something new if put together. Two old ideas could merge into a fresh, groundbreaking one if fused in the right way. Two stages of a process may be melded into one to create a more streamlined, efficient procedure.

Questions that can facilitate this line of thinking include the following: "Can we put two or more elements together?" "Can we carry out two processes at the same time?" "Can we join forces with another company to improve our market strength?"

For instance, the combination of the spoon and fork has led to the innovation of the spork, a utensil now often packed within ready-to-eat noodle cups because of its cost-saving and convenient design. It solves the problem of having to manufacture two different utensils and effectively halves the cost of production.

Adapt. This technique intends to adjust something in order to enhance it. It solves problems by improving on how things are typically done, with adjustments ranging from something small to something radical. It challenges you to think of ways you can alter what's already existing—be it a product, a process, or a manner of doing things—such that it solves a current problem and is better tailored to your needs.

Noticing that you have less energy than usual, for instance, you may think of solving the problem by making adjustments to your food choices, such as cutting back on empty calories and processed food. In the business world, this technique is often utilized by brainstorming groups looking to enhance their product, service, or production process.

Some questions considered under this rubric include the following: "How can we regulate the existing process to save us more time?" "How can we tweak the existing product to sell better?" "How can we adjust the existing process to be more cost-effective?"

An example of an adaptation for a product is the development of mobile phone cases that have been imbued with shock absorbers or shockproof material. This clever tweak has obviously been developed in response to the common problem of accidentally dropping and consequently damaging fragile phone parts. In a similar vein, waterproofing mobile phone cases, wristwatches, and the like is another instance of adapting a product in order to improve it.

Magnify or minimize. This technique involves either increasing or decreasing an element to trigger new ideas and solutions. Magnifying pertains to increasing something, such as exaggerating a problem (for perspective), putting more emphasis on an idea, making a product bigger or stronger, or doing a process more frequently.

On the other hand, minimizing entails decreasing something, such as toning down a problem, deemphasizing an idea, reducing the size of a product, or carrying out a process less frequently. Thinking about either magnifying or minimizing certain elements is bound to give you fresh insights as to the most and least significant parts of your problem, thus guiding you toward effective solutions.

Discussion questions that apply the magnify technique include the following: "How can you exaggerate or overstate the problem?" "What would be the outcome if you emphasized this feature?" "Will doing the process more frequently make a difference?" As for minimizing, challenge yourself to ponder the following: "How will playing down this feature change the outcome?" "How can we condense this product?" "Will doing this step less frequently lead to better efficiency?"

Say that you've been assigned to transfer to a smaller office. You now have the problem of fitting your things into a more confined space. Using the magnify and minimize technique to resolve your dilemma, you can ask yourself which office components you want to place more or less emphasis on. Are you going to place more importance on having space for receiving and meeting with clients, or for tech equipment or maybe for file storage?

Mulling over which aspect to magnify will help you pick out and arrange things in your new office in a way that best reflects your needs and values. As for using the minimize technique, consider which of your office stuff may be condensed to fit a smaller floor area. For example, while previously you may have had separate tables for your computer and your printer, you may think of using a compact computer desk with a printer shelf instead.

Put to another use. This technique aims to figure out how an existing product or process may be used for a purpose other than its current one. It stimulates a discussion on the myriad of other ways you might find a use for anything from raw materials to finished products to discarded waste. It's basically about finding a new purpose for old things.

Some questions that can facilitate this line of thinking include the following: "How else can this product be used?" "Can another part of the company use this material?"

"Can we find a use for the bits we throw out?"

Consider how this would apply to stuff lying around in your own home. For instance, how would you address the problem of old newspapers just piling up in a corner? Using them to clean your windowpanes is a common solution, but how about finding other fresh ways to use them? By challenging yourself to think of more unconventional uses, you will magnify the way those old newspapers benefit you, from serving as trusty deodorizers for shoes to being raw materials for fun papier-mâché crafts.

Eliminate. This technique refers to identifying the unnecessary elements of a project or process so that they can be eliminated and thus provide for an improved outcome. It considers how a procedure may be streamlined by dropping redundant steps or how the same output may be produced despite cutting resources. Whatever resource is freed up may then be used to enhance creativity and innovation.

Questions that make up this rubric include the following: "Is there any step we can remove without affecting the outcome?" "How would we carry out the same activity if we had half the resources?" "What would happen if we eliminated this part?"

One of the most useful applications of this technique is in the area of addressing financial problems in daily life. For example, you find that you're earning enough for your daily expenses but never get to put money aside for emergencies. Barring the option of gaining more income, the only thing left to do is to subtract expenses so you can save for an emergency fund.

Using the eliminate technique, identify expenses you can cut—maybe pass up on buying that shiny new bag you don't really need, or opt for cheaper home-cooked meals instead of dining out. The money freed up from eliminating unnecessary expenses can then be your savings for rainy days.

Reverse. This technique suggests switching up the order of the process steps in order to find solutions and maximize innovative potentials. Also known as the rearrange technique, this line of thinking encourages interchanging elements or considering the process backward in order to stimulate a fresh take on the situation.

Some questions that apply the reverse technique include the following: "How would reversing the process change the outcome?" "What would happen if we carried out the procedure backward?" "Can we interchange one step with another?"

Say you're having trouble fulfilling your personal promise to exercise more. You've had it written in your schedule to spend thirty minutes exercising at the end of the day. But when it comes time for it, you always seem to have other more urgent things to attend to or are too tired for it. Thus, you never get around to doing it consistently. To solve this problem, you may consider applying the reverse technique.

Check whether you may interchange your exercise time slot with another part of your day, such as making time for it first thing in the morning instead. By reversing the time you set for exercising, you may just find it easier to stick to the routine, as in the morning you're not yet drained or overwhelmed by the day's activities.

The SCAMPER method is one of the easiest yet most effective strategies for finding solutions to problems and sparking creative thinking. Because a process is explored from seven different perspectives—substitute, combine, adapt, modify, put to another use, eliminate, and reverse—no stone is left unturned, and even unconventional solutions can be uncovered.

By forcing you to think in a specific, unique way, the SCAMPER method jolts your mind out of its regular pattern and onto new roads worth exploring. And for every new path you explore, you generate innovative and varied ideas, creating a pool from which you can later draw the best solution to solve the problem at hand. Where you had one or two ways of looking at a problem, you now have seven additional approaches to apply.

The next technique for more creative and divergent thinking is similar to the C portion of SCAMPER.

Take, Borrow, Steal

It sounds sinister, but the truth is, most creative and innovative thought comes from something else. And if it doesn't, that's the first place you should look for inspiration. Though it's likely you've seen this phenomenon in many instances, it has been officially called the *Medici effect* by author Frans Johansson. He describes the Medici effect as the emergence of new ideas and creative solutions when different backgrounds and disciplines come together.

The term is derived from the 15th-century Medici family, who helped usher in the Renaissance by bringing together artists, writers, philosophers, mathematicians, and other creatives from all over the world.

Arguably, the Renaissance was a result of the exchange of ideas between these different groups all in close proximity with each other in 15th-century Florence and Rome.

Johansson proposes that in the modern business world as well, the Medici effect is the key to best meeting client needs and maximizing profits while minimizing costs. Believing that all new ideas come from merging existing ideas in creative ways, he recommends utilizing a mix of backgrounds, experiences, and expertise in staffing to bring about the best possible solutions, perspectives, and innovations in business. Take what works well in each discipline and marry them.

And the same holds true for creativity in general as well—pulling in knowledge from different disciplines and relating elements from various fields are powerful tools for generating creative ideas. A common object in one field may be an extraordinary tool in another. A perspective or approach might be commonplace in one discipline but revolutionary in another. A conventional concept in one domain may have new and interesting applications in a different one.

For example, creative implementations of traffic rules have pulled ideas from not only electronics, engineering, and information technology but also from visual arts, psychology, and advertising. It's a familiar concept in psychology that people, when making decisions, rely on not only rational information but also emotional cues. Utilized in implementing traffic laws, this concept has led to the innovation of using smiley faces in traffic lights to get more people to respond to them.

The advantages offered by pulling together knowledge and resources from multiple disciplines to aid problem-solving are evident in the findings of researcher and professor Brian Uzzi. Analyzing over 26 million scientific papers published over the last several centuries, Professor Uzzi found that the most impactful have been those done by teams with members from an atypical combination of backgrounds.

Another of his investigations revealed that top-performing studies cited an atypical combination of other studies, often pulling in at least 10 percent of their citations from fields other than their own.

Thus, to be creative, you'll need to evoke the Medici effect by broadening your perspective to encompass different disciplines and not being afraid to wander outside your current area of focus. Poke your nose into other fields and pull from them ideas that might work in combination with what you already have. By bringing in knowledge from other disciplines, you introduce a fresh take on your creative venture and give yourself the best chance of coming up with remarkable innovations and solutions.

It is perhaps no coincidence that we still speak of Leonardo da Vinci and his polymathic tendencies—perhaps our continued regard is due to those very tendencies. At the very least, he was an accomplished painter, sculptor, engineer, architect, and anatomist. He also possessed keen interests in ornithology, machinery, and ciphers. He is the prime example of how different disciplines can come together, synergize, and spit out creative work that is revolutionary and innovative. It is also no coincidence that the Medici family was one of da Vinci's prime patrons during his lifetime.

Albert Einstein also utilized this concept in his method of *combinatory play*.

Though Einstein is not traditionally known for his creativity, there can be no doubt that a scientist with outrageous and innovative theories possesses a massive degree of creativity. It's not just following a set of equations that can lead to scientific breakthroughs—a mindset full of openness and a determination to find the unknown is required, and Einstein certainly had those in spades.

You probably know the basics of Einstein's intellectual accomplishments—for instance, the theory of relativity and a newfound understanding of the laws of physics. But you may not know how he was able to come to these discoveries.

The most notable scientist of the 20th century was known for taking time out of his research to play the violin. Reportedly, he was even very good at it, as he was with the piano. But while sawing away on the violin during his breaks, Einstein actually arrived at some breakthroughs in his research and philosophical questionings. Allegedly one of these musical sessions was the spark for his most famous equation: $E=mc^2$.

Einstein came up with the term "combinatory play" to describe the intangible process in which his favorite pastime led to ideas that revolutionized the whole of scientific thought. He explained his reasoning as best he could in 1945 in a letter to French mathematician Jacques S. Hadamard:

"My Dear Colleague:

In the following, I am trying to answer in brief your questions as well as I am able. I am not satisfied myself with those answers, and I am willing to answer more questions if you believe this could be of any advantage for the very interesting and difficult work you have undertaken.

(A) The words or the language, as they are written or spoken, do not seem to play any role in my mechanism of thought. The psychical entities which seem to serve as elements in thought are certain signs and more or less clear images which can be "voluntarily" reproduced and combined.

There is, of course, a certain connection between those elements and relevant logical concepts. It is also clear that the desire to arrive finally at logically connected concepts is the emotional basis of this rather vague play with the above-mentioned elements. But taken from a psychological viewpoint, this combinatory play seems to be the essential feature in productive thought—before there is any connection with logical construction in words or other kinds of signs which can be communicated to others.

(B) The above-mentioned elements are, in my case, of visual and some of muscular type. Conventional words or other signs have to be sought for laboriously only in a secondary stage, when the mentioned associative play is sufficiently established and can be reproduced at will.

(C) According to what has been said, the play with the mentioned elements is aimed to be analogous to certain logical connections one is searching for.

(D) Visual and motor. In a stage when words intervene at all, they are, in my case, purely auditive, but they interfere only in a secondary stage, as already mentioned.

(E) It seems to me that what you call full consciousness is a limit case which can never be fully accomplished. This seems to be connected with the fact called the narrowness of consciousness (Enge des Bewusstseins)."

As this letter inidicates, Einstein seemed to believe that indulging in his creative tendencies was helpful for his logical and rational pursuits.

Combinatory play is not simply the notion that *play* takes your mind to a different world to regroup. It recognizes, as Einstein did, that taking pieces of knowledge and insight from different disciplines and combining them in new contexts is how most creativity truly happens. So as mentioned, Einstein achieved something in playing the violin that helped him think about physics in an entirely new way.

The lesson here is to engage in your own pursuits and not feel constrained by having to stay in similar or adjacent disciplines, thinking that they will aid you. There are *always* parallels between different disciplines, so find them. More of the same probably will not help; a dash of something different just might.

Einstein became well-known for another thinking technique, and it is one that we use most days in everyday life.

"What if humans were capable of flying?"

"What if the world's landmasses never broke up into separate continents and instead remained as Pangaea to this day?"

These are hypothetical "what if" questions that tickle your mind into thinking from other perspectives and challenge you to question your premises. Imagining hypotheticals goes beyond simple thinking skills that require only memorization, description of an observable event or situation, or even analysis of facts and concrete events. Because hypotheticals pose questions about what isn't, what hasn't happened, or what isn't likely to ever happen, they stretch the imagination in new ways and sharpen creative thinking and practical intelligence. Again, this is similar to how SCAMPER forces new possibilities.

For instance, you've never considered the implications of human flight because it's impossible, so there is a world of thoughts that have remained unexplored. How would traffic lights work, what kind of licensing process would be required, would we still have cars and airplanes, and how would safety work? Now, how would those rules and laws apply to normal traffic situations in the present day? Think through the realities of how everything would fit together—it's no small feat!

Hypothetical situations taken to the extreme are thought experiments, and Albert Einstein in particular was known to use these. He called them *Gedankenexperiments*, which is German for "thought experiments."

A thought experiment, in a more general context, is essentially playing out a "what if" scenario to its end. It's acting as if a theory or hypothesis were true, diving deep into the ramifications and seeing what happens to your "what if" under intense scrutiny. A thought experiment allows you to analyze interesting premises you could never manifest in reality and make new leaps of logic and discovery because you can consider conditions that current knowledge doesn't yet reach.

Suppose the problem situation is needing to exit a room. The conventional ways to do so are to walk out the door or jump out the window. But what if the door is blocked by a raging fire and the room is on the tenth floor of the building? These conditions have now rendered your conventional solutions fatal. You can only get out of the room either by finding a way to kill that fire or by having the capacity to survive a fall of several hundred feet. Something in this scenario needs to drastically change its usage or definition, or it will break entirely. This is the essence of the thought experiment. *Suppose this happens. What happens next? And then? And then?*

Thought experiments were one of Einstein's superpowers. He could imagine a scenario, play it out mentally with shocking accuracy and detail, and then extract the subtle conclusions that lay within.

One of Einstein's most famous *Gedankenexperiments* begins with a simple premise: what would happen if you chased and then eventually caught up to and rode a beam of light through space? In theory, once you caught up to the beam of light, it would appear to be frozen next to you because you are moving at the same speed. Just like if you are walking at the same pace as a car driving next to you, there is no acceleration (the relative velocities are the same), so the car would seem to be stuck to your side.

The only problem was that this was an impossible proposition at the turn of the century. If you catch up to the light and the light appears to be frozen right next to you, then it is inherently impossible that it is light, because of the difference in speeds. It ceases to be light at that moment. This means one of the rules of physics was broken or disproved with this elementary thought.

Therefore, one of the assumptions that underlay physics at the time had to change, and Einstein realized that the assumption of time as a constant had to shift. This discovery directly laid the path for the theory of relativity. The closer you get to the speed the light, the more time becomes different for you—relative to an outside observer.

This thought experiment allowed Einstein to challenge what were thought to be set-in-stone rules set forth by Isaac Newton's three laws of energy and matter. This thought experiment was instrumental in realizing that people should have questioned old models and fundamental "rules" instead of trying to conform their theories to them.

Thinking More "Plainly"

The third tactic for creativity is to get back to the basics. When we think of creativity, we often conjure visions of elaborate and complex masterpieces that are one of a kind. But while these masterpieces are indeed products of creativity, we often make the mistake of thinking that the process of creating them also required complex and elaborate thought. We fail to recognize that while the product may look intricate, the process that created it may have first required simplicity in thinking.

Thinking more plainly means zooming out and gaining a looser perspective on things. It's being able to grasp the gist of the problem rather than getting stuck on its minute details. You think in terms of goals and not in terms of process. It sounds confusing, but a simple example is to replace problem-specific verbs with generic ones when stating the problem. For instance, don't ask, "How could I *drive* something over a long distance?" Instead, think, "How could I *move* something over a long distance?"

Moving covers not just driving but also flying, swimming, sliding, throwing, crawling into a catapult, and more. Using the looser, more generic verb "move" opens up more possibilities because it removes the restrictions of the specific verb "drive." A study by Clement and colleagues demonstrated how such a technique can dramatically improve performance in tasks requiring analogical thinking. They found that when problems were described in more generic terms, the participants' performance improved by over 100 percent in some tasks.

So if you're tackling a creative task or problem, write it down and highlight or circle the verbs and keywords you used. Then consider if there's a more general umbrella term those words belong under and opt to use the more general term instead. With your task now phrased in a more generic way, rethink the possibilities considering this new formulation.

Thinking more plainly encourages rapid idea generation because by considering matters in more universal terms, you also widen your view of what's possible. The wider your playground, the more areas you have for play and discovery. One of the biggest hindrances to idea generation is when you limit your thinking to a small area only, which is exactly what happens when you phrase the task in specific terms instead of general ones. You start to get tunnel vision and fail to see the variables and givens actually present in the situation. Such a perspective severely limits your options and thus also hinders you from generating ideas and creative solutions for your problem.

In the same way, seeing only the specific, common uses of things is another major obstacle to creativity. Known as "functional fixedness," this creativity-blocker surfaces when you have everything you need to solve the problem, but you can't do it because you see only the usual or traditional function of the objects you have. You get stuck (i.e., "fixed") on that sole specific function of the object, so you're inhibited from thinking of any more creative uses for it to help you in your current situation.

Psychologist Tom McCaffrey demonstrates this concept by setting the two-rings problem, which challenges participants to fasten together two heavy steel rings with only the following: a two-inch steel cube, a long candle, and a match. He adds the condition that melted wax would not be strong enough to secure the rings together.

The solution to the problem requires an escape from functional fixedness. You would first need to get past the view of the candle's usual function and recognize that its wick is not just for burning, but is also a piece of string you can use to fasten things together. If you allowed yourself to fixate on the common, specific function of a candle, then you would be inhibited from using it to solve your problem.

Thus, the key to generating solutions is to escape the trap of functional fixedness by thinking of objects in more generic terms. To this end, McCaffrey developed the *generic parts technique*. This technique involves first breaking things down into their component parts with more generic descriptions (e.g., a candle has a wick, which qualifies as a string in general), then asking yourself how you can use that component to solve the problem (e.g., how having a string can help you out). So again, it's by thinking more plainly in such generic descriptions that you move toward generating effective solutions and creative ideas.

So the next time you want to come up with more creative ideas, think in simpler, more general, and universal terms. For instance, instead of thinking how you would *paint* your store walls to be more interesting, consider how you would *make* those walls interesting. The more general term "make" opens up more possibilities for your creativity to run wild, going beyond just brushing paint onto a wall and instead leading you to experiment with other materials, textures, and techniques to make that wall truly one of a kind.

Idea Box

Finally, as many masters of creativity know, creativity is less about making new ideas from scratch and more about forging new connections among already existing ideas, materials, and techniques. This tactic helps you do exactly the latter, in an organized and systematic way, so that you don't miss any opportunity to spot an interesting connection wherever it may arise. Called the idea box, this method involves constructing a grid that helps you have a clear picture of the possibilities and potential areas of innovation no matter what your creative project may be.

To construct your own idea box, first enumerate the essential parameters of the product or service you want to generate ideas on. This builds on other concepts for idea generation, notably combination and methodical lists. For example, you're trying to invent a new home item. Some parameters you may include are location, shape, material, and purpose. Write these parameters at the topmost row of your grid, like so:

	Location	Shape	Material	Purpose
1				
2				
3				
4				

Next, list down the different variations or options under each parameter. For location, for instance, you may write down living room, kitchen, bedroom, and bathroom. In the same way, list different variations of each parameter under their respective columns:

	Location	Shape	Material	Purpose
1	Living room	Cube	Wood	Storage
2	Kitchen	Round	Metal	Decoration
3	Bedroom	Elongated	Plastic	Organization
4	Bathroom	Irregular	Glass	Functional tool

After you've completely filled out your grid, it's time to generate those ideas! Pick out one option per parameter and conceptualize how the four might be *combined* to create your new home item. For example, combine bathroom (location), irregular (shape), glass (material), and organization (purpose).

Merge these four elements in your mind and let your creativity flow. You want something that's made of glass, irregularly shaped, and used to organize things in the bathroom. Is there a vision forming in your head? What object are you imagining? Maybe you begin to visualize an interesting star-shaped glass cupboard you can affix to the wall, with each of the star's spikes holding a different type of bath item, toiletries, or other supplies. This is just one possible combination you can create with the four-by-four idea box above—and using such a grid, you have a total of 254 potential ideas at your fingertips.

Idea boxes are typically four-by-four grids, such as the example above, or often have six-by-six dimensions. For your own idea box, you may have more parameters and options as you see fit, with each addition yielding exponentially more ideas and solutions. As you randomly combine the different variations of your parameters, you stimulate your mind to use combinations you've never considered before. The idea box is a way to generate loads of ideas in an organized and systematic manner. So challenge yourself to use all the variations in your box, such that you force your thinking beyond the comfortable and the obvious in order to generate truly unique and innovative outcomes. Also remember to avoid evaluating and critiquing your ideas at this stage; just let them flow freely and in all possible directions.

Takeaways:

- Divergent thinking is mostly known as creative thinking. It's the process of looking outside and beyond what you currently have and coming up with new thoughts. This stands in contrast with convergent thinking, which is the act of evaluating what you currently possess. How does this process relate to practical intelligence? It's the act of problem-solving and making do with what's in front of you.
- The SCAMPER method forces you to think in foreign and novel directions. It stands for (S) substitute, (C) combine, (A) adapt, (M) minimize/magnify, (P) put to another use, (E) eliminate, and (R) reverse. It utilizes the general concept of force fitting, which is when

you force unfamiliar concepts and ideas together mentally, thereby creating necessarily new patterns of thought.
- Understand that the best creative thinking will draw upon different fields and disciplines. What is novel is one discipline is natural and worn in another. One of the best examples of this is Einstein's combinatory play, which interweaves logical and creative thought—as a mental break, or through combining the two thought processes. Einstein's other contribution to creative thinking is in his usage of thought experiments and playing out hypotheticals in detail to their logical conclusion.
- To get more creative, think more plainly. It sounds counterintuitive, but simple thoughts underlie complex processes and solutions. Thinking more basically allows you to refocus on what matters and escape what is known as *functional fixedness*. When we start to view goals and concepts in isolation and free of contextual constraints, we are freed.

- Finally, try out an idea box. It's a methodical way for you to rapidly generate a massive amount of ideas geared toward the exact problem you want to solve. It's similar to the SCAMPER method because it very clearly and visually encourages force fitting.

Chapter 5. The (Un)Limited Brain

Humans have physical limitations, and we know this instinctually. If someone has a race or competition coming up, we know to suggest to rest up. If someone is tasked with running a marathon, we're aware that we can't just tell them to "tough it out." Any time a challenge is coming, someone will tell you, "Try to go to sleep early the night before!"

It's like we can imagine tangible sweat, toil, and effort from a physical act, and thus understand it. The physical body will break down at some point—perhaps later than you might expect, but it is not without limits.

But when it comes to our mental abilities, most of us tend to ignore the concept of limitations. You'll hear things such as "mind over matter" or "just use your willpower," as if the brain is capable of perpetual motion without a break. While these sayings are helpful in the context of motivation and cultivation of self-discipline, they must be qualified when we consider the goals of this book—mental agility, smarter thinking, and insightful analysis.

Most people—teachers, professors, and authors alike—want to push the notion of the unlimited mind. But from my perspective, it's more important to first understand how the mind is *limited*, and thus, how we can work with the inherent restrictions we are facing.

Let's consider the example of Devon. Devon loves to procrastinate, and he's been this way since he was a child. He blames his love for video games, which has resulted in unhealthy weekends where he barely leaves his home, subsisting only on Cheetos, Mountain Dew soda, and whatever else is on hand to eat.

This habit followed him into college and then his career as a marketing analyst. He routinely pulled all-nighters to finish his tasks and assignments, often taking the next few days to recover and chip away at his accumulating sleep debt. His daily routine involves staying up until 4:00 a.m. and waking up at 7:00 a.m. After a time, the quality of his assignments and reports begins to suffer at his job. He starts getting negative reports of his lack of energy and engagement in the office during the day. To compensate, he spends even more late nights trying to polish his work, but that just leads to more overall fatigue without an improvement in the work quality.

Devon's story culminates when he is driving to work one inauspicious Tuesday morning and hits a police car because he is so drowsy. It's a stark illustration of our mental limitations. We would never recommend that an athlete partake in a training schedule like Devon's, but we fail to consider the impact lack of rest has on our thinking abilities. Smart thinking, though it may not always seem like it, correlates directly with our physiology and how optimized the rest of our bodies are. If you view the human body like a machine, a machine can't function properly without sufficient fuel or with a single faulty component.

Smarter thinking does not equal *harder* thinking.

Thus, this final chapter on practical intelligence is about the preconditions to doing so—how we must nurture our bodies in order to nurture our brains. To think at our sharpest, we need our bodies to be at their healthiest.

If you want to stick to the nitty-gritty details of how to think smarter and view the world with a different lens, you can feel free to skip this chapter. But I wouldn't recommend it. In fact, this should probably be the first chapter, but sometimes I find it's more compelling to start with the *how* versus the *why*.

This chapter gives an overview of the complex machine that is the human body. The first step to harnessing your brain for practical intelligence is to understand the circadian rhythm that governs our daily energy.

Circadian Rhythms

If you don't have energy, you won't have the will to even attempt to think smarter. You will be stuck in bed eating ice cream and reverting to the path of least resistance, which is lazy and surface thinking. Energy is the most important part of maximizing your thinking abilities and alertness. Just as a track athlete needs adequate sleep and nutrition before a race, you need energy for any degree of insight.

From a biological standpoint, each person has a finite amount of energy available on a daily basis, so understanding your body's rest and wake cycles will help you determine how to allocate your mental energy.

You know from personal experience that your energy level varies throughout the day. No one operates at a high energy level 100 percent of the time. You've probably experienced the mid-afternoon food coma, which usually occurs a couple hours after lunch. It is possible to circumvent the body's natural rhythms through use of stimulants, such as caffeine, but inevitably, the artificially high-energy period is followed by a crash when the body insists on compensating for the lack of rest.

Energy management is about understanding how your body functions and working within those limitations instead of fighting them. You can't be 100 percent alert and insightful 100 percent of the time, but you can be strategic about when you try.

We are all governed by a natural energy cycle called the *circadian rhythm.* It's why we get jet lag and can't adjust to new time zones very easily—we have set periods of rest and activity that are dictated by our biology.

Sleep researcher Neil Kleitman identified the presence and importance of rapid eye movement (REM) sleep, and discovered that the body generally operates in ninety-minute cycles, moving progressively through periods of higher and lower alertness. In other words, our energy and alertness come in ninety-minute chunks. These ninety-minute cycles apply whether we are awake or asleep, and we can use this information in a few ways.

First, we now know there is essentially a time limit to productive thinking. It's not endless; in fact, it might be capped at ninety minutes at a time. At the end of an intense ninety-minute work period, we grow fatigued and begin relying on stress hormones for energy. Recall the last time you pushed yourself mentally and how you might have felt "wired" in some way.

Then, suffering from overload, the prefrontal cortex begins to shut down, and we move into fight-or-flight mode. We may attempt to override the body's signals by fueling ourselves with caffeine and sugar, but in the end, our focus and concentration suffer.

Research from both Peretz Lavie and the U.S. Army Research Institute back up these findings, stating unequivocally that following our natural circadian rhythms of ninety-minute work periods followed by a short rest allows us to maintain stronger focus and higher energy levels throughout the day.

The point here is to listen to your body. It is telling you exactly how it prefers to function. When you sit down to work, you have a ticking time bomb of ninety minutes before you lose peak motivation and focus. This deadline can obviously vary between individuals, but the proposal that our thinking abilities come in bursts applies to everyone.

Besides creating ninety-minute cycles, the circadian rhythm also distributes these peaks and dips of energy throughout a twenty-four-hour period in specific ways. There are specific times when you can maximize your thinking, and others when you are setting yourself up for failure. Of course, keep in mind these are averages, and outliers do exist.

As we move through a typical day, it takes a few hours after waking to reach our peak levels of energy and alertness. For many people, the late-morning hours, after 10:00 a.m., represent the highest period of mental sharpness and focus. This is when you might take advantage of your brain functioning at its peak. But remember, you probably have only ninety minutes on average to do so.

Soon after lunch, our energy levels begin to decline.

According to Christopher Barnes's writing in the *Harvard Business Review*, your turkey sandwich isn't to blame (although your daily cycles can be affected by a wide variety of stimuli, including the type of food you eat). Our body's energy naturally dips somewhere between 2:00 and 3:00 p.m., possibly because we are at the midpoint of our wake cycle. For thousands of years, humans have rested during the afternoon (think of the Spanish concept of the midday *siesta* or nap), and only since the Industrial Revolution imposed an emphasis on mass productivity have we begun to eliminate this critical period of rest for the nine-to-five workday.

After we hit that afternoon dip, our energy levels begin rising again, and we generally hit our second peak around 6:00 p.m. As the evening wears on, our energy diminishes, slowly transitioning into sleep cycles.

The typical circadian pattern is very common, but individuals may exhibit significant differences. Sometimes the rhythm is shifted toward a specific time of day. Morning people, characterized as *larks*, tend to have energy peaks earlier in the day than the average person, while night people, called *owls*, are at their most effective after the sun goes down.

The circadian rhythm is something that rules our day-to-day existence. You can fight it, but why would you? Work within the simple guideline it lays out for your energy, and you will find that smarter thinking becomes the rule rather than the exception.

The next piece of the puzzle in thinking smarter is the general well-being of your physical body. Remember, if the machine is broken down in any way, functionality will be compromised.

Stress, Sleep, and Exercise

Just like an athlete and her physical body, the brain must be ready for performance, and the factors of stress, sleep, and exercise greatly influence that. For the most part, these elements are within your control, which makes them even more important. Let's begin our mini-tour of how neurological health is directly correlated to your brain's functioning.

Stress is one of the biggest influences on the brain's health. If you want a clear and concrete illustration, you don't have to look any further than any veteran or trauma victim suffering from post-traumatic stress disorder (PTSD) and how their lives are negatively affected. These people literally lack the ability to function in daily life because they are so tense, and they are likely to snap at any given moment as an outlet for their anxiety and fear.

A plethora of research has found that stress impacts the brain's health and mental capacity in hugely negative ways. This is in large part due to the body's physiological response to stress. But first, it will be helpful to define the difference between the two main types of stress: chronic and acute stress.

Chronic stress is when you are under ongoing stress for a relatively long period of time—something as small as being under a constant heavy load at work, or dealing with a relationship that is frequently combative. These are small sources of stress that seem insignificant until you look at the cumulative effects and realize you are always on edge, testy, and tense with knots in your shoulders. When we are experiencing chronic stress (the amount of which is highly variable and relative to the person's tolerance), our body is in a state of physiological arousal. This is known as the fight-or-flight response, and it's our body's main defense mechanism when it senses a stressor.

This mechanism was useful millennia ago when the terms "fight" and "flight" were truly taken literally—if the body sensed a stressor or a reason to be in fear, it would put itself on the highest levels of alertness and be prepared for a fight to the death, if necessary, or running away as quickly as possible. In either case, the body's hormones, heart rate, and blood pressure are highly elevated. The main stress hormone, cortisol, is released in spades and has been implicated in causing the alertness.

So if you are under chronic stress, you are permanently in this fight-or-flight mode of alertness and have an overload of cortisol. Your body will very rarely reach the relaxation phase, which is known as a state of homeostasis. And unfortunately, cortisol impedes your mental abilities with regard to risk analysis.

In other words, chronic stress makes you alert and physiologically aroused *all the time*. This is exhausting both physically and mentally, and has the effect of shrinking your brain. Studies have shown that chronic stress has caused as big as a 14 percent decrease in hippocampal volume (the area of your brain responsible for memory encoding and storage), which is startling.

A study (Pasquali, 2006) showed that memory in rats was negatively affected when the rats were exposed to cats, which presumably caused stress. The rats that were exposed to cats more routinely were unable to locate certain entrances and exits of their enclosure.

The difficult part of this situation is you may not realize you are under chronic stress, because it has become normalized for you. It is just like when your shoulders tense up—you probably don't realize it until someone points it out and you can see the contrast between being relaxed and being tense.

The cumulative effects of being constantly on edge, paranoid, unable to focus, and feeling despair and overwhelmed will catch up to you. Imagine being pumped up on adrenaline for days, weeks, or months. Not only will it impair your memory and brain processing, it will leave you unable to function in general. Excess and consistent cortisol can cause a loss of neurons in the prefrontal cortex and hippocampus, as well as decrease the neurotransmitter serotonin, which is what creates the feeling of *happiness*. This is what people with PTSD suffer, but to a much higher degree.

Acute stress, on the other hand, is not something that will slide by unnoticed.

Acute stress is the sudden jolt of adrenaline you experience when someone cuts you off in traffic and you nearly crash, or you get into a heated argument. However, acute stress is momentary, temporary, and you can feel it and notice it. This is when adrenaline is coursing through your veins, leaving your palms sweaty and hands shaking. Your body is trying to give you the alertness and strength you need for anything. Intense bouts of acute stress can even cause headaches, muscle tension, upset stomachs, or vomiting.

If this type of stress persists for a longer period of time, it just may cross the threshold into chronic stress.

But the labels are unimportant. What's important is what happens to your brain's abilities when you are under any type of stress. You can also think of the brain as simply being occupied with thoughts of stress and anxiety, so much so that it is unable to divert brainpower to thinking clearly. This wouldn't be an inaccurate characterization of the role of stress.

The next part of the healthy brain equation is sleep. It has long been argued that specific modes of sleep are where memories are actually created and where learning can be said to occur. It is thought that the brain's structure is changed and synaptic connections are formed during sleep.

Indeed, studies have teased out the specifics of how memories are enhanced or stored during sleep. In a 2005 study, Professor Matthew Walker of Harvard University was able to compare fMRI scans of the brains of subjects while awake and asleep to see the different parts of the brain that were activated—where memory consolidation occurred. He found that people's cerebellums were far more active after a period of sleep between periods of learning, and this activity was highly correlated with better learning and memory.

Professor Walker commented, "Sleep appears to play a key role in human development. At twelve months of age, infants are in an almost constant state of motor skill learning, coordinating their limbs and digits in a variety of routines. They have an immense amount of new material to consolidate, and consequently, this intensive period of learning may demand a great deal of sleep."

Specifically, rapid eye movement (REM) sleep is most important for memory consolidation and storage during sleep. There has been debate in recent years about just how important it is to memory, but sleep can also serve another purpose: we sleep to forget the unimportant facets of our day and filter them out so our memories can become more organized.

In 2003, research conducted at the University of Wisconsin-Madison hypothesized that neurons and synapses essentially worked and proliferated in overload during the day, and were pruned back during sleep so only the important information made it into longer-term memory. This implies that we sleep to literally forget certain parts of our day and to have better-organized memory.

A team of researchers from the University of Rochester have also posited that sleep is like the brain's "waste removal system." When you can provide the systems responsible for memory a reprieve overnight, it is simply likely they will continue to work better for you in the coming days.

Sleep can serve many specific purposes for the brain and memory, but overall, the brain, like the body, needs rest and recovery. This is not even mentioning the deleterious effects of sleep deprivation, where one set of researchers from the University of California, Los Angeles, likened a lack of sleep to drinking too much. Patients with epilepsy were studied, and they were found to have a litany of ongoing issues: memory lapses, distorted visual perception, impaired and sluggish thought, and a slow reaction time. From the description alone, this sounds like someone who has had a few too many alcoholic drinks. Think of sleep as ongoing maintenance for the machine of your brain.

The final piece of the puzzle is exercise. It might be surprising to hear that physical exercise is just as good for your brain as it is for your muscles and bones, but it's been proven time and time again.

One particular study was conducted at Radboud University in the Netherlands. Male and female subjects took a memory test, and then one third of them exercised immediately after the test, one third of them exercised four hours after the test, and the remaining third did not exercise at all following the test. The subjects were collected two days later to repeat the same memory test, and the group who exercised four hours after the initial test performed the best without fail. It appeared that exercise was effective in helping the brain stabilize and store the memory.

Other studies take the physiological angle and point to the neurotransmitters and hormones that exercise releases and how they affect memory processes. Exercise is instrumental in the production of a brain protein called FNDC5, which eventually releases brain-derived neurotrophic factor (BDNF). BDNF has been shown to aid general brain functioning and memory processing by preserving existing brain cells, promoting the development of new brain cells, and encouraging overall brain growth. Human brains tend to shrink when we grow older, but exercise, which creates BDNF, can literally increase the size of your brain.

Your brain primarily uses glucose (what carbohydrates are converted into) for fuel, and when that is not available, it begins to use fat for fuel. It is when the brain starts to use fat for fuel that BDNF creation is triggered. This is possibly behind the science of fasting and why low-carbohydrate diets have been shown to report high amounts of alertness and cognitive acuity as pleasant side effects (Fond, 2012).

Your brain has the highest oxygen requirement of any organ in your body, up to 20 percent of your entire body's usage. When you can exercise and improve your cardiovascular system and ensure that blood is pumping more effectively through your arteries, you will have greater access to oxygen. The same holds true with water—the brain is, on average, 70 percent water, and exercise makes you more aware of hydration.

Exercise does have its limits, however. The best types of exercise are those that increase blood flow and burn fat. If exercise becomes too strenuous and difficult, then you begin to create stress, and you've already read how detrimental stress can be on your mental faculties. Overall, it appears that the maxim of healthy body, healthy mind holds very true.

It's just another case of why we should have listened to our mothers more when we were young.

Sleep as much as possible, exercise often, and don't sweat the small things. When we can avoid the stressors in our life, we can devote more mental bandwidth to that which matters. You wouldn't do a great job studying for a test if your dog was missing, would you? We can better comprehend and understand difficult material when we have a full night's sleep and nothing distressing on our mind. Finally, exercise is not only invigorating and important for giving you a mental break, but it can cause chemical changes in the brain that benefit your memory processes. The brain is the engine of learning and expertise, and you have to be mindful of priming it for optimal performance.

The Need for Less

Burnout is a very real risk, especially in today's modern age where everyone is always seeking ways to get ahead of the competition. It seems that everyone has a full-time job as well as a *side hustle* that is aimed toward making money. We seek to intentionally pack our days full of activities, professional and social, as a means of squeezing the last drop of enjoyment out of our lives. *Busy* is a state that is often romanticized and sought after.

Ironically, this tendency quickly becomes counterproductive, because very few people have a motor that can function like that. As for what that means for your brain, any shred of fatigue will affect your clarity of thought. That consequence should be clear from earlier parts of this chapter, as well as our own lives. We function better on eight hours of sleep versus three hours of sleep.

We all probably have an idea of what burnout is, but it is typically characterized by physical exhaustion, detachment and apathy, anxiety, and a lack of focus or attention. It can be difficult to catch, because it tends to build slowly over time. Recall our discussion of chronic stress—burnout functions in a similar way and forces persistent levels of cortisol in the brain. Subjects in Swedish studies on burnout showed two surprising traits: enlarged amygdalae and thinning of the prefrontal cortices. Respectively, these are associated with strong and uncontrolled emotional responses (outbursts, perhaps), and prematurely aging (and worse-functioning) brains.

Burnout goes beyond ignoring our circadian rhythms or pulling the occasional all-nighter. This is what happens when you push your brain to the limits again and again without proper recovery. As a reminder, you would never consider doing this with any type of athlete. Burnout is damaging and sometimes has long-term effects. Sometimes, the best thing we can do in thinking smarter is *nothing*.

Disconnecting from everything and simply doing nothing at all is an integral part of quick and insightful thinking. Breaks are a necessary evil to thinking smarter, and sometimes a break is the most productive thing you can do.

A break allows you to regain your focus and gain fresh perspective, because the brain is always up to something, even during rest.

Rest puts your brain into a type of thought known as *diffuse thought*—this is where you are not focusing on anything in particular, and it stands in contrast to *focused thought*, which is when you are thinking with one goal or intention. Diffuse thought is when your conscious mind is relaxed and your thoughts wander freely and make connections between unrelated information and topics. You might refer to this as "zoning out" or "turning your brain off."

Consider that focused thought is like a flashlight with a highly concentrated beam of light, while diffuse thought is like a wider and dimmer beam of light. They emphasize different types of attention: deep analysis and thought on a limited set of information, versus shallower analysis and thought on a wider variety of information. Thus, diffuse thought has been shown to be highly useful in problem-solving or creative thinking.

Perhaps most importantly, a break allows *alpha brainwaves* to generate.

There's a reason that when we are zoning out without anything specific to focus on, such as when we're in the shower, we seem to have a disproportionate amount of epiphanies. Thinking is inherently fatiguing and taxing on the mind, and is characterized by the brain emitting *beta brainwaves*. Relaxation and a lack of focused attention, on the other hand, is characterized by the brain emitting *alpha brainwaves*.

Beta brainwaves allow us to focus and think clearly, but too much will lead to stress and anxiety. They are associated with alertness and arousal. Alpha brainwaves calm us down and provide much-needed recovery. In a study published in the journal *Cortex*, alpha brainwaves have also been found to boost creativity by an average of 7.4 percent. In the same study, it was also found that people with depression have impaired alpha activity; thus, it wouldn't be inaccurate to say that alpha brainwaves are associated with better moods and overall greater happiness.

Additional studies by Professor Flavio Frohlich have also shown that alpha waves are associated with enhanced memory, creative thinking, and overall increased mood.

Maybe that's the reason meditation and mindfulness are touted as a cure-all, justified or not. They intentionally slow you down and put you into a state of releasing alpha waves, which triggers increased feelings of happiness and life satisfaction. Many of the world's top performers, such as CEOs and elite athletes, mention meditation as a vital part of their daily routine, and this is likely why. The ability to tune things out allows them to function at their peak when it matters, like a battery recharge in the middle of the day.

We instinctively know to sleep, stretch, and warm up our bodies if we have an athletic competition, but we disregard doing the same for our minds. When you relax and do nothing at all, you enter a state of allowing your mind to wander, and you also come back recharged and refreshed. It might help to think of it as part of the work process.

Fuel Yourself

Finally, the machine of the human body is nothing without proper and sufficient fuel. Here is some quick math to convince you of the importance of fueling your brain properly with nutrients and water.

The human brain uses roughly 20 percent of the caloric energy that you consume. This is despite the fact that the brain makes up only about 2 percent of your body weight. The brain is *hungry*, and you need to make sure to feed it sufficiently; otherwise, your performance will dip all too easily. If you don't give yourself adequate nutrients, or you don't continually hydrate yourself, your brain is what will suffer the most (proportionally, at least).

The simple math makes it clear that we need to keep our brains fueled to stay in peak working condition. Something that is under debate is the frequency with which we should refuel ourselves—with food, anyway.

Many recent studies have espoused the benefits of intermittent fasting on mental alertness and clarity. Intermittent fasting is a state of eating separated by periods of fasting—not eating. A daily schedule for this might look something like skipping breakfast and then eating all of the day's calories between noon and nine at night only, and repeating this process the next day. To some, this might go against the conventional wisdom of eating a hearty breakfast, or something similar to the saying of "eat like a king in the morning, a rich man in the afternoon, and a beggar at night."

But the studies speak for themselves. Intermittent fasting has been shown to induce neurogenesis, which is the growth of new neurons in the brain (Manzanero, 2014). It has also been shown to reduce inflammation in both the body and the brain (Lavin, 2011); to produce more BDNF, the wonder hormone from earlier in this chapter (Liou, 2010); to make people more energetic and alert because of how it affects the cell structure of the mitochondria (Jornayvaz, 2010); and intermittent fasting has even been demonstrated to increase metabolism from 3 to 14 percent (Mansell, 1990).

But this isn't a book about intermittent fasting or espousing specific eating patterns. The point is that what we put into our bodies—the fuel—makes a large impact on our ability to think clearly, even the time and method of the fuel. It benefits our brain health overall and can help keep us alert because of how much energy our brains consume.

You might be wondering what you should eat, for brain health specifically. Harvard University Medical School makes some general recommendations, and they focus on omega-3 fatty acids, saturated fats, B vitamins, and antioxidants. More specific recommendations include green leafy vegetables for the vitamin K and lutein, berries for flavonoids (which have been shown in a 2012 study to improve memory), nuts, and moderate doses of caffeine.

Of course, the other component of fuel is *water*.

Water there is zero debate over. Being dehydrated significantly reduces your mental performance and brain health. More simple math: remember, our brains are 70 percent water. They get affected the most when you are in a state of dehydration. A UK study found that ninety minutes of sweating without additional hydration shrinks the brain as much as a year of aging or almost three months of Alzheimer's Disease (Kempton, 2011). Another study suggested that driving while dehydrated can be similar to driving drunk because of the decrease in focus and reaction time, as well as impaired motor skills (Loughborough University, 2012)

When it comes to dehydration, there is very little margin for error, as well. Significant detriments to analytical thought, short-term memory, long-term memory recall, problem-solving, and general cognitive performance were found in just a 1 percent level of dehydration (Riebl, 2013).

Thus, drink more water throughout the day for smarter thinking. Don't rely on *feeling* thirsty to understand that you need more water. Preempt this, because the thirst response does not activate until you are already dehydrated, and it will be too late by that point. Take a proactive approach to drinking more water and account for weather, environmental conditions, or other factors that would necessitate greater intake. The old maxim of "eight glasses of water a day" may not be accurate or even necessary, but you probably need more water than you are currently getting—at least for optimal brain performance.

Drink more water than you think you should and you're on the right track to keeping your body fueled for practical intelligence.

Takeaways:

- Unfortunately, human brains are not entities capable of perpetual motion. In fact, they are flesh and blood and require all the considerations of the muscles of an athlete. This is all to say that the best mental performance and thinking has a set of preconditions—a fueled and rested physical body. Without our flesh engines being properly prepared, practical intelligence is only a fantasy.
- Our energy is generally ruled by the circadian rhythm, which governs how long we can focus (about ninety minutes) and when we are prone to focusing (late morning and early evening) and resting during the day. There are limits both in terms of frequency and duration in the course of a single day.
- The roles of stress, sleep, and exercise are heavily underrated for mental performance. If you are under either chronic or acute stress, your brain will be fueled by cortisol and be focused on risk detection versus analytical thought. If you are sleep deprived, your memory

and mental "waste removal system" will be compromised, and your functioning will begin to mirror that of a drunk person's. Exercise helps increase blood flow to the brain and creates what is known as BDNF.

- The brain also needs a break from time to time; otherwise, there is a very real risk for burnout. Besides short-term feelings of apathy and disinterest in anything at all, burnout can create long-term effects of decreased emotional regulation and brain shrinkage. Rest and recovery have the added benefits of summoning diffuse thought (creating connections between information) and alpha brainwaves (calm, relaxing, increased creativity and mood).
- The final piece of brain health en route to optimal thinking is what we fuel ourselves with. Food and water, of course. Feed your hungry brain, whether you do it through three traditional meals a day or intermittent fasting. What to eat is of relatively less importance. Drink more water than you might feel necessary, because even a 1 percent rate

of dehydration has been shown to cause lower cognitive performance across a variety of tasks.

Summary Guide

Chapter 1. Look Beneath the Surface

- Practical intelligence is another way of saying common sense, but we all know that common sense truly is not so common. One of the key lessons to learn with practical intelligence is that nothing is what it seems at first glance. The world doesn't readily reveal itself nakedly to you, so it's up to you to look beneath the surface to understand what you see. We want to do this, but we are too often driven by certainty and speed instead of actual truth.

- The first and most natural way to probe below the surface is through cultivating curiosity. There are five types of curiosity, each of which can be said to be a motivation for asking questions: joyous exploration, deprivation sensitivity, stress tolerance, social curiosity, and thrill-seeking. However, curiosity will rarely come easily or naturally, especially about things that we don't have an innate interest in. So we need to generate that same approach through other methods.

- One methodical way to seek truth and simulate curiosity is by embracing skepticism. No, it's not about being *cynical* or simply refusing to believe what people tell you. Rather, it's refusing to blindly believe what people tell you, and requiring evidence and facts. In this way, a skeptic is quite similar to a scientist utilizing the scientific method. No answer is required here, and only understanding is sought. Skepticism requires slowing down your thoughts and thinking like a scientist.

- Finally, we come to critical thinking. Critical thinking is concerned with questioning answers rather than asking questions. It seeks to take nothing at face value and provide a three-dimensional and nuanced view of a topic or stance. Without that, you are by definition jumping to conclusions or relying on someone else's word—an opinion without inquiry is a weak one. We can practice critical thinking through a series of questions, but we can also go a level deeper by running inquiries and thoughts through the Paul-Elder framework of critical thinking. This involves three components that ultimately work together to build a bulletproof thinking process: (1) elements of thought and reasoning, (2) intellectual standards to be applied to these elements, and (3) the cultivation and eventual development of intellectual traits.

Chapter 2. Watch Yourself

- This chapter has a tall task—to get you to think about your thinking. When we're not engaging in what is known as metacognition, it's easy to veer off the path of clear thought. You must become aware of your thought patterns and where you tend to stray. Watch yourself and try to evaluate what's happening inside your brain.

- This process begins with System 1 and 2 thinking, as conceived by Daniel Kahneman. System 1 thinking is quick, instinctual, and decisive—and also often incorrect. System 2 thinking is measured, calm, and analytical—and far slower and more difficult. Unfortunately, the brain operates on the principle of least resistance, so while System 1 thinking is first and foremost, we want to get into the habit of System 2 thinking on a consistent basis. The easier and more familiar a task becomes, the more instinctual and quick it can be, so the way to clearer thinking is consistent repetition and practice.

- Cognitive biases are a similar concept, where we leap to conclusions because they appear to fit schema or heuristics we are familiar with, or are simply in line with our personal experiences. These can also be effective, but often wrong. Notable biases include: availability heuristic (I can remember it, so that means it is important), gambler's fallacy (X happened, which means Y must happen), post-purchase rationalization (I made a good decision . . .), and confirmation bias (I only read what I want to read).

- How can you overcome cognitive biases, aside from simple awareness and metacognition? There are four keys: alternative explanations and reverse storytelling, rewording statements and assumptions as questions, getting behind your implicit assumptions, and removing pride and ego from the equation.

- Finally, it's important to understand logical arguments—and especially illogical arguments. We hear these every day but may not be able to pick out their logical flaws. You can think of these as a combination of math and argumentation that allows us to see the reality versus what you see or hear. There is the conditional statement (X -> Y, true), the converse statement (Y -> X, usually a flaw), the inverse statement (Not X ->

Not Y, usually a flaw), and the contrapositive statement (Not Y -> Not X, true). It's not just word games; it's understanding the foundations upon which real and false arguments are built.

Chapter 3. Think in Models

- One of the best ways to embody practical intelligence is Charlie Munger's concept of mental models. These are heuristics, or handy rules of thumb, for how to approach situations in smart ways. It's when we try to freelance everything in our lives that we truly run into trouble, so having (relatively) universal guidelines or blueprints for how to act intelligently and efficiently can be invaluable.

- Among the innumerable approaches that exist, we talk about the Pareto Principle (80/20 ratio), thinking about secondary consequences, distinguishing between feeling and thinking, satisficing (satisfy + suffice), prioritizing motion over planning, and addressing Murphy's

Law (whatever can go wrong, will go wrong).

- Three mental models are specifically suited toward our purpose of practical intelligence and acting within the bounds of common sense. First, we discuss the difference between evaluating a process versus an outcome. Often we can fall into the trap of outcome bias, wherein we ignore our decision process simply because something turned out favorably. Second, we learn to tell stories in reverse using the fishbone diagram analysis. This is a powerful tool to deal with the problem of cause and effect and illuminate our thinking to the possibilities of alternative perspectives. Third, we come to separating correlation from causation, and understanding the true relationships between events we observe.

Chapter 4: Thought Divergence

- Divergent thinking is mostly known as creative thinking. It's the process of looking outside and beyond what you currently have and coming up with new thoughts. This stands in contrast with convergent thinking, which is the act of evaluating what you currently possess. How does this process relate to practical intelligence? It's the act of problem-solving and making do with what's in front of you.

- The SCAMPER method forces you to think in foreign and novel directions. It stands for (S) substitute, (C) combine, (A) adapt, (M) minimize/magnify, (P) put to another use, (E) eliminate, and (R) reverse. It utilizes the general concept of force fitting, which is when you force unfamiliar concepts and ideas together mentally, thereby creating necessarily new patterns of thought.
- Understand that the best creative thinking will draw upon different fields and disciplines. What is novel is one discipline is natural and worn in another. One of the best examples of this is Einstein's combinatory play, which interweaves logical and creative thought—as a mental break, or through

combining the two thought processes. Einstein's other contribution to creative thinking is in his usage of thought experiments and playing out hypotheticals in detail to their logical conclusion.
- To get more creative, think more plainly. It sounds counterintuitive, but simple thoughts underlie complex processes and solutions. Thinking more basically allows you to refocus on what matters and escape what is known as *functional fixedness*. When we start to view goals and concepts in isolation and free of contextual constraints, we are freed.
- Finally, try out an idea box. It's a methodical way for you to rapidly generate a massive amount of ideas geared toward the exact problem you want to solve. It's similar to the SCAMPER method because it very clearly and visually encourages force fitting.

Chapter 5. The (Un)Limited Brain

- Unfortunately, human brains are not entities capable of perpetual motion. In fact, they are flesh and blood and require all the considerations of the muscles of an athlete. This is all to say that the best mental performance and thinking has a set of preconditions—a fueled and rested physical body. Without our flesh engines being properly prepared, practical intelligence is only a fantasy.
- Our energy is generally ruled by the circadian rhythm, which governs how long we can focus (about ninety minutes) and when we are prone to focusing (late morning and early evening) and resting during the day. There are limits both in terms of frequency and duration in the course of a single day.
- The roles of stress, sleep, and exercise are heavily underrated for mental performance. If you are under either chronic or acute stress, your brain will be fueled by cortisol and be focused on

risk detection versus analytical thought. If you are sleep deprived, your memory and mental "waste removal system" will be compromised, and your functioning will begin to mirror that of a drunk person's. Exercise helps increase blood flow to the brain and creates what is known as BDNF.

- The brain also needs a break from time to time; otherwise, there is a very real risk for burnout. Besides short-term feelings of apathy and disinterest in anything at all, burnout can create long-term effects of decreased emotional regulation and brain shrinkage. Rest and recovery have the added benefits of summoning diffuse thought (creating connections between information) and alpha brainwaves (calm, relaxing, increased creativity and mood).
- The final piece of brain health en route to optimal thinking is what we fuel ourselves with. Food and water, of course. Feed your hungry brain, whether you do it through three traditional meals a day or intermittent fasting. What to eat is of relatively less importance. Drink

more water than you might feel necessary, because even a 1 percent rate of dehydration has been shown to cause lower cognitive performance across a variety of tasks.

www.ingramcontent.com/pod-product-compliance
Lightning Source LLC
Chambersburg PA
CBHW071155070526
44584CB00019B/2803